Prepared Companions

Prepared Companions

The communication manual
for loving relationships

Forewords by
DAVID OLSON, PH.D.
CAROL MATUSICKY, PH.D.

DR. ROBERT LEES

A PAC PAN Book

This book published simultaneously in the United States of America and in Canada.

Copyright © 1993 by Robert Lees

Canadian Cataloguing in Publication Data
    Lees, Rob.
        Prepared companions

        Includes bibliographical references and index.
        ISBN 0-9697151-0-2

        1. Intimacy (Psychology)   2. Interpersonal
    relations. I. Title
    BF575.I5l43 1993   158' .2   C93-091766-9

Quantity Purchases

Quantity purchases are eligible for special terms when ordering this title. For information, write: Group Sales Department, PAC PAN PRESS INC.

In Canada: 15611 Pacific Avenue, White Rock, B.C. V4B 1S1
In the U.S.:   1733 H Street, Suite 330-738, Blaine, WA 98230

Cover and Book Design by John Barson

Manufactured in Canada
September 1993

FIRST PRINTING

For information on workshops, speaking engagements or interviews by Dr. Lees call:
Integra Counseling Group Inc. (604) 792-9690

Table of Contents

PERSONALITY ISSUES

REALISTIC EXPECTATIONS

COMMUNICATION

COMMUNICATION

CONFLICT RESOLUTION

SEXUALITY

SPIRITUALITY

FAMILY BACKGROUNDS

FAMILY & FRIENDS

FINANCIAL RESPONSIBILITY

EQUALITARIAN ROLES

CHILDREN & PARENTING

PERPLEXING PROBLEMS, TROUBLING TIMES

ACKNOWLEDGEMENTS

Special thanks are due to Fraser Valley Broadcasters: President, Bill Coombes, STAR FM station manager, Barry MacMaster; and production managers Neal Forsythe and Marc North for their support of the radio features that formed the basis of this book. Also, John Barson of The Changing Family radio program and Pac Pan Press who was responsible for the layout, technical development, cover design and publishing of the manuscript. John's irrepressible desire to help families by providing useful, non-sensational information was an inspiration which saw the project through to completion. Thanks go also to Donna Williams, Linda Brotherston, and Carol Lees for the use of their gifts as professional educators in providing editorial review of the manuscript.

FOREWORD

PREPARED COMPANIONS is for all couples who want to better understand each other, improve their communication and develop a more intimate relationship. Rob Lees has written a very insightful and valuable book on a wide range of important relationship issues for couples, incorporating numerous clinical insights from years of experience working with both premarital and married couples.

He has designed this book around the *PREPARE* Inventory which is a couple questionnaire developed by my colleagues and I. *PREPARE* contains several important relationship categories with about 10 items for each category. These relationship areas include the major topic areas for the book including: *Personality Issues, Realistic Expectations, Communication, Conflict Resolution, Sexuality, Spirituality, Family Background, Family & Friends, Financial Responsibility, Equalitarian Roles, and Children & Parenting.*

The 100 issues discussed by Rob Lees were drawn, for the most part, from the specific items in the *PREPARE* Inventory. These are highly relevant issues for couples who want to learn more about their relationship.

This book can be a valuable resource for any person in a couple relationship. It can be even more valuable when used in conjunction with the *PREPARE* Inventory. While *PREPARE* can help to identify both strengths and growth areas for couples, this book can provide a wealth of useful ideas regarding how to resolve issues that arise in the relationship. PREPARED COMPANIONS is a great book for anyone who wants to develop and maintain an intimate relationship.

David H. Olson, Ph.D.

David H. Olson, Ph.D. is Professor, Family Social Science, University of Minnesota, 290 McNeal Hall, St. Paul, MN. He is also President of PREPARE/ENRICH, P.O. Box 190, Minneapolis, MN 55440

Every so often a book comes along and fills a much needed niche. PREPARED COMPANIONS is a superb book - long overdue and a welcome resource in the lives of busy couples. Most of us, whether beginning a relationship or in an intimate relationship want that relationship to work well. There are few guideposts out there to help us along the way. We expect more of our intimate relationships and often can not find the encouragement and wisdom we need to keep our relationships alive, nourished, and growing. PREPARED COMPAN-IONS is a book that I envision as having a permanent place in every couple's bedroom. It is the kind of book that says, "Take time-out for yourselves. It's worth it!"

Written in an easy-to-read style, PREPARED COMPANIONS is based on sound research and on the personal and professional experience of Dr. Rob Lees in his extensive work in psychology and marriage and family therapy. This is a book of insight and practical wisdom. It is a book to be bought, not borrowed. I highly recommend PREPARED COMPANIONS. Don't leave home without it!

Carol Matusicky, Ph.D.

Carol Matusicky, Ph.D. is Executive Director of the British Columbia Council for the Family, Vancouver, B.C. Canada

INTRODUCTION

This book was written for any person who is preparing for or is in an intimate relationship. Although it was originally intended for couples preparing for marriage, I discovered that the articles contained in the book appealed to a wide cross section of society. They were first written as radio scripts for a brief feature on family relations, and since I have found that they are useful in many surprising ways. Elderly parents wanted copies to share with their married children. People struggling in long term marriages reported that these texts were confirming and at times enriching. Through listener feedback, I realized that the material was broad enough to appeal to a wide audience.

Relationships of the 1990's are similar, yet different, from intimate relationships of any other generation. These articles comment on some of the new stresses facing relationships while hopefully providing some time honoured wisdom. They point to ways that couples can survive and thrive. The positions taken in the articles are based on my years of experience as a psychologist/marriage and family therapist and my keen interest in family social science literature.

Inspiration for the book came from *PREPARE,* an instrument created for couples by Dr. David Olson of the University of Minnesota. Dr. Olson is one of the world's foremost authorities on family social science. *PREPARE* has become one of the most frequently used tools for marriage preparation. Items from *PREPARE* provided a starting point for many of the articles. Although no book or instrument can cover every issue couples might face, *PREPARE* and this book touch a broad cross section of the most important marital concerns.

Knowledge does not create a happy marriage. It does however help people clarify what they want and how they might get it. There is empirical evidence that sound marriage preparation prevents divorce. Where it doesn't prevent divorce, it often softens the impact of changing relationships. It is hoped that this book will contribute to these efforts.

Dr. Robert Lees

Personality
Issues

JEALOUSY

Suppose you love someone and he or she seems to be jealous. Likely you know about this jealousy in a variety of ways, from your partner becoming silent and pouting when you're out in mixed company, to your partner doing embarrassing, attention-getting things. When you go out with friends or become involved in organizations that your partner is not a part of you hear complaints. In extreme cases of jealousy, you are accused of being unfaithful . . . almost to the point where you want to be unfaithful out of sheer anger and defiance. Being on the receiving end of someone's jealousy is usually not pleasant. At first it can be deceiving. It can seem flattering to have someone want you so much that they feel threatened when they don't have your undivided attention. This soon wears thin and begins to feel stifling and controlling. So what can a person do when they are on the receiving end of jealousy? First, there isn't a lot that you can do, because it is usually someone else's problem which is affecting you. The important thing is not to start to own the problem. You can, however, analyze your own behaviour and motives to see if they are appropriate. Do you inadvertently or perhaps intentionally act in provocative, flirtatious ways? Get some feedback from others on this. You might also consider what is appropriate in terms of the stage of your relationship.

An important step in dealing with jealousy is to encourage an open, sensitive exploration of these kinds of feelings.

If you are just dating someone, then you should feel the freedom to go out without them. If you are engaged or married, you might want to reconsider going to a dance without your partner. If it turns out, after considering the stage of the relationship and your own behaviour, that you are acting reasonably, then it will be important for you to confront the issue of jealousy with your partner on an adult-to-adult basis. Start by trying to understand the root of your partner's jealousy. Usually it's based on lack of trust, insecurity, poor self-esteem and fear of loss. An important step in dealing with jealousy is to encourage an open, sensitive exploration of these kinds of feelings. Put yourself in your partner's place and try to understand his or her insecurity. Maybe a little more affirmation from you will help. Maybe it might take a few behaviour modifications, such as holding your partners hand when in new social situations, or sitting with your partner when at a dance, instead of skipping from table to table. If you can make a few modifications that will help your partner, then do it. But be careful that you do not start accommodating or giving in to the jealous behaviour in a way that puts unhealthy restrictions on your life. If the problem doesn't seem to be improving, urge your partner to get professional help, so that the green-eyed "jealousy monster" does not consume your relationship.

THE TEMPER

Jane is concerned about Allen's temper. It seems that at times he goes almost right out of control. She becomes frightened and feels alienated. When the temper is raging "Allen" has left. Jane doesn't know him any more. When the anger subsides, he's loveable again, but it's not as easy as before to love loveable Allen. In fact, many of the things Allen says in anger cut deep. They may be forgiven, but they aren't forgotten. Like a drunk who doesn't remember what was said the night before, Allen acts as if everything should return to normal. It never does. Jane and Allen have a serious problem. To help resolve it, they need what therapists call "meta-communication." Meta-communication is communication about how we communicate. Jane or Allen could start this. They would need to begin this communication analysis in a place where they will remain "adult," civil and in control of their emotions and at a time when both are rested, fed and without the influence of alcohol or drugs... a public place, like a restaurant would be appropriate. Or, maybe Allen and Jane could communicate through letters where each could think and reflect before responding to what their partner has to say. Or, this analysis might be done in a counselling office. Both partners will need to face how "the temper" could destroy a love they cherish. In a spirit of trust and vulnerability, they both need to reveal their feelings about "the temper."

Remember, one of the first rules of human behaviour is, "behaviour positively reinforced is behaviour that will re-occur."

Jane likely feels hurt and frightened; Allen likely feels guilty, ashamed and afraid that he is pushing her away. He's likely in a vicious cycle, whereby he gets frustrated with himself for letting "the temper" take control of him. This feeds his rage and it is more likely that "the temper" will explode in the relationship once again. If there is one essential thing that Jane needs to do in this situation, it is to not back down to "temper" or to let "temper" have its way. This would only encourage it. Wonderful "making ups" after a bout of temper, unfortunately, often act to reinforce the inappropriate behaviour. Certain personalities are more volatile and intense. However, this is never a legitimate excuse for emotional, verbal or physical abuse. A person like Allen will need to confront his own rage and the "temper" that manifests it. Raging can result from childhood injury or it may simply be the result of having used it as an effective strategy for getting his way in past relationships. One thing is clear: it will not go away unless Allen takes responsibility for it. Allen needs to realize that most people feel rage, at times, but not everyone deals with it through temper tantrums. Anger management programs, personal therapy, or will power gained through meta-communication can quell this destructive behaviour.

7

IF YOUR PARTNER SEEMS DEPRESSED

Within every intimate relationship, there comes a time when one partner becomes worried about the mental health of the other. This can take the form of being concerned that your partner is under too much stress, or reach the extreme of worrying about your partner's perception of reality. The most common mental health problem in North America is depression, so it isn't surprising that at one time or another a marital partner will be concerned that his or her partner is depressed and down. It is important to know that some personalities gravitate towards the darker side of life. In the movie "City Slickers," the friends of the main character bet that he couldn't go more than 30 minutes without talking about death. Certainly some of the greatest thinkers and personalities throughout time have been melancholic types. This is a natural part of every person's personality structure. However, some have more melancholia than others. It isn't something you can ask these people to change. If you don't like it, you need to ask yourself if it's your problem or theirs. On the other hand, you may notice that your partner's mood seems different than the norm for them. In this case, the thing to do is to describe and then ask the meaning of this behaviour. Don't jump to conclusions. Just report what you see.

Depression is one of the most curable of mental illnesses. It is usually a matter of finding the right treatment for the right person.

In one case a woman thought for years that her husband was depressed. When she mentioned this, he said that he was just "thinking deeply." This simple explanation enlightened and relieved her a great deal. Depression can be seen in negative behavioural, emotional and thinking changes. Usually there is a shift in sleep and eating patterns and an abandonment of creative activities for more passive activities like television watching or drinking. Often there is sadness and negative attributions about life and oneself. If you recognize these kinds of changes in your partner, the thing to do is to ask about them. Tell them with examples just what you see that concerns you. Sometimes simply talking a problem through can alleviate a mild depressive mood. If this doesn't help, professional assistance should be encouraged. The important thing is to confront the problem. It might involve medication, or medication in combination with individual or interpersonal therapy. Remember that depression is an understandable condition that can be overcome. The helping role you can play is to encourage your partner find the treatment that works.

CONFLICT OVER DRUGS & ALCOHOL

onflicts over the amount a partner smokes, drinks or uses drugs, can often be the undoing of a relationship. Consider this couple - she is a health professional who sees the destruction of drug and alcohol abuse in the course of her work. She becomes anxious when her partner drinks at parties. Noticing her noticing his drinking, he becomes defensive. When they talk about it he assures her that he doesn't need a second mother. His defensiveness leads her to feel misunderstood and to worry more. Drug and alcohol dependencies are often progressive diseases. They grow gradually and take families by surprise. Very often they shouldn't be a surprise. They may even be predicted on the basis of family background, your partner's personality profile, preferred way of dealing with problems and methods of seeking gratification. The ideal would be for every couple planning to be married to think about their family's history with drugs and alcohol. If there has been a pattern of misuse of these substances, they should ask themselves what they would like to have as the norm in their relationship. Obvious problems are created when a couple adopts a lifestyle where drugs and alcohol are frequent companions. High alcohol and drug usage are correlated with health and social problems.

Do everything you can to avoid talking like a parent to a child.

As well, where a couple has manifested a high-usage relationship with drugs and alcohol and one partner chooses to move towards a healthier lifestyle, the marital equilibrium is upset. The most common example of this would be the young mother who decides to give up drinking and smoking because she is pregnant. Her new sense of responsibility likely will not coexist well with the couple's established relationship to drugs and alcohol. As with most relationship problems, the key action here is to confront the issue, not your partner. Non-blaming statements of your perception, coupled with your feelings about the problem, can help to reduce negative reaction from your partner. Do everything you can to avoid talking like a parent to a child. Stick with the evidence, your feelings about the evidence and your logical concerns. If your partner reacts defensively given this presentation, his or her response may indicate this really is a problem. If your partner promises to change and nothing happens, this may be indicative of more serious problems. At this point, it may be necessary to consult others who love and care for this person and together consider seeking professional advice. Do not leave this kind of issue to fester too long. The earlier you intervene, the more likely a successful resolution.

WHEN YOUR PARTNER IS UNDEPENDABLE

J udy thinks Tom is irresponsible and undependable. When they first met, she was attracted by his boyish ways, his love of fun, his sports car . . . but now things have changed. They are married, have a home and a child . . . now his sportscar, his parties, his toys, make him appear to be a "big kid." In Judy's mind, Tom never assumes enough responsibility for their home and their child. She finds herself reminding him of these things. Tom and Judy have the makings of a common pathological relationship pattern; unfortunately it is one that still receives some support from societal role models - the "mother/ son marriage." Usually, it is the woman who is encouraged to be overly responsible for home and family. In some cases, it is the man. Whichever way, it ends up something like this: the more Judy nags Tom, the more childish he acts; or is it that the more childish Tom acts, the more Judy nags? Obviously these two people are caught in a relationship dynamic that exerts a force which shapes their behaviour. Eventually, tragically, Tom and Judy separate. Tom wants equal access to their son. Judy cannot believe this. "He never wanted to take on responsibility when we were together!" She, with cause, distrusts him.

If you find yourself in one of these over-competent/under-competent, dependable/undependable relationships, it is important to remember that these are relationship roles and not personality traits. The same person in a different relationship may play a different role.

This means that when Tom and Judy divorce, Tom may very well act far more responsibly and adult than she thought possible. In fact, this is a common scenario, where the so-called "Peter Pan Man" surprises everyone by growing up. Could Tom and Judy have changed their relationship and stayed together? Likely they could have done so. This would probably require change in behaviour on both parts. Judy, angry and convinced of Tom's undependability, may have overlooked many of the "dependable" things Tom did, while exaggerating those things she understood to be signs of irresponsibility. Her perception attribution acted like blinders. Tom could have confronted Judy's anger. Rather than react with counter anger to her frustration, he could have, in a rational "adult" voice, pointed out when he felt patronized or "parented" by Judy. Realizing the consequences of the resentment and anger associated with this relationship pattern, plus the high emotional costs of divorce, Tom and Judy may have engaged in frank negotiation on their relationship expectations. If together, they can challenge and attempt to change the communication pattern, and not each other, they stand a good chance of keeping their love alive and their marriage together.

BEING EMBARRASSED BY YOUR PARTNER'S BEHAVIOUR

The art of successful relationships is determined by having enough attachment to feel close to someone else, while maintaining an appropriate distance that allows each of you to have your unique personality. Consider these two differing personality styles that are frequently attracted to each other - the "dramatic" and the "conscientious." The dramatic personality is outgoing and loves an audience. The conscientious personality is usually more reserved, conservative and introverted. Think of how they function at a party. The dramatic partner will likely be vivacious, in the centre of things, the life of the party. In contrast, his conscientious partner stays in the corner talking with the same person all night, looking unhappy and never budging from her chair. There will be times that the conscientious partner will be embarrassed by the attention seeking of the dramatic partner. She might be angered at her dramatic partner's gregariousness, which might appear as flirtation. She might think that her partner is drinking too much, talking too loud, or acting silly. This couple will likely have a conflict about when to leave the party, with the conscientious one watching the clock with one eye, and her partner with the other. On the other hand, the partner with the dramatic personality might feel annoyance every time he notices his partner sitting like a lump in the corner.

If you are bothered by your partner's behaviour, it may be that your own identity is too enmeshed with his or hers, that you consider your partner to be an extension of yourself.

He might feel embarrassed by his more demure partner's refusal to join the frivolity. In some cases he will have wished he came alone, that somehow his partner's lack of involvement is a weight on him. He may believe she has restricted his own personality, but resent his partner for "having to do it." The dynamics in these relationships point to the need for something which psychologists refer to by a number of different names: detachment, differentiation, or individuation. If you are bothered by your partner's behaviour, it may be that your own identity is too enmeshed with his or hers, that you consider your partner to be an extension of yourself. Thus, if he or she does something that you won't do, you are judging them by the standards of behaviour you set for yourself. It means that you aren't really free to be yourself when you are out in public with your partner. It may be that if you feel embarrassed by your partner in public, you have a serious relationship problem. It may, however, be indicative of a problem you have with your own identity. Your goal should be to be comfortable with yourself as you are, giving your partner the freedom to be who he or she is.

DEALING WITH STUBBORNNESS

Flexibility is a key element in the survival of many creatures and institutions-marriage is one of them. Unfortunately, there are those who have difficulty making transitions or adapting to new situations. Some of us experience this same kind of stubbornness only at particular times or in particular interactions. Whenever it appears, stubbornness can be very hard on relationships. Think of what it is like to be stubborn. You don't want to budge from your position. You don't want to change. You feel forces pushing against you to have you do something you don't want to do. Stubbornness is digging in your heels in a way that indicates NO ROOM FOR NEGOTIATION. The heart of it lies in a desire to maintain some control and therefore, it is often associated with a fear of change. In relationships, stubbornness can emerge in a variety of ways. Your partner wants you to go to church with them once a month; you refuse. Your partner wants you to stay at a party until the end rather than be the first ones to leave; you say you won't go then. Your partner wants to take a holiday this year rather than continue to put all your holiday savings into the mortgage; you insist that there will be no holiday until the mortgage is paid, twenty years from now.

If you are known as a stubborn person, it would be important to look at the effects of this on the people you love.

You can see from these examples that your partner would feel shut out or "excluded" by your insistence on having things your way. Without negotiation, there is no relationship. If you are known as a stubborn person, it would be important to look at the effects of this on the people you love. A common response to stubbornness is anger. Anger often leads to blame and an atmosphere of distrust. In this environment, it is unlikely that any meaningful sensitivity for feelings and the position of the other, or for creative compromise, will take place. Certain personality styles gravitate towards stubbornness. It is important to know this so that you can get yourself out of thinking that your partner is being stubborn purposefully to bug you. Once you stop personalizing stubbornness, you can begin to understand it. Once you understand it, you can influence it. In what ways does stubbornness serve as a useful defense mechanism? What is the stubbornness protecting? Ask the stubborn one this question. "What is it that keeps you from considering this other option?" "What do you think would happen if you did?" Stubbornness can destroy relationships. Taking the time to question further the reasons behind the stubbornness can lead to a much better understanding of the core personality features of your partner.

LIVING WITH NEGATIVISM

I n a classic textbook on the psychology of religion, *The Varieties of Religious Experience*, William James, an early American psychologist, wrote of two types of people: first born and second born. According to James' typology, first born people have an innate optimistic personality. They would always see the glass as half full, the bright side of a difficult situation. Second born are people with a deeper awareness of the darker side of life: they tend towards pessimism, melancholia and enjoy Woody Allan movies. James called them second born, because to get past their negativism and darkness, often they needed to experience the religious equivalent of a "second birth." What James was pointing to was that some people, by virtue of personality, not conscious choice, have a predisposition towards negativism. These are our social critics, our prophets. Their intensity and passion make them attractive, but difficult to live with. At times, it is simply enough to know and respect differences; at other times negativism can be a problem. Consider this scenario. Bill comes home from work to find the kids have their toys out all around the living room. Although Sharon has been busy all day, the laundry isn't done and dinner isn't ready. Bill growls at the children, complains about the tough day he had and moans about supper never being ready on time. Can you imagine what this feels like for Sharon? Bill can't. But if Sharon doesn't confront Bill with this, she will become turned off. Then Bill will become even more grumpy, because he won't feel loved.

We need to know when to simply accept our partners, and when to challenge them.

Critical people often feel estranged and need to feel respected and loved. However, as with many of the other difficult personality traits, negativism should not be accommodated. That means Sharon should not scurry around before Bill gets home to clean up the toys so Bill won't be upset. Instead, Sharon needs to help Bill to confront his negativity. As with any other relationship problem, this is best handled at a time when both parties have the time and ability to reflect. Sharon could say, "Bill, I want to bring up something that has been affecting my feelings for you. Do you mind if we talk about it, because I want to get it out of the way?" Notice three important elements in Sharon's approach to Bill. She asked his permission to talk about the problem. She "owned" the problem, thus helping Bill to avoid a defensive posture and she stated her intention to get the problem out of the way so she could get closer to Bill. The scenario of the negative spouse is typical of the sensitivity we need to be successful in relationships. We need to know when to simply accept our partners, and when to challenge them.

WHAT TO DO WITH A MOODY MATE

Everybody is entitled to a bad day once in awhile, but for some people, fluctuations in mood is a part of a frustration pattern for themselves and even more so for those who love them. Mood fluctuations, being really "up" one day and in the dumps the next, can be a part of an enduring personality pattern, or be one of the psychiatric disorders known as "mood disorders." Probably the best known among these is manic-depression, or bipolar, disorder. A more common and less severe kind of manic-depression is cyclothymia. Cyclothymia is sort of like having a little bit of manic-depression. These problems are often addressed with medication. Another popularized mood problem is PMS, premenstrual syndrome. The literature on these conditions makes it clear that a large part of our mood has to do with biochemical changes. This is important to understand so that loved ones can get past personalizing this behaviour, such as "You always act this way just to bug me!" This doesn't mean, though, that you should not have your loved one be responsible for managing his or her mood. There are also those people whose changes in mood are simply a part of their personality structure. Whatever the cause, living with a moody person might seem like being on a roller coaster.

Addressing this moodiness together will assuredly make you a stronger, closer couple.

Loved ones need to learn to distance themselves from these moods and to develop a hands off policy when it comes to attempting to change what may be so central to this person's being. If you have a loved one who seems to be moody, you might have to begin to address your own feelings about this before you start to begin to raise it with them. Have you taken these mood changes personally, assumed it was your fault, assumed that they were done on purpose to hurt you? It would be important to stop personalizing the problem so that you can more accurately document what it is you are seeing. The next step would be to approach your partner about it, asking him or her if the variability in moods is noticed and if so, how he or she feels about it. It is important to do this in a non-blaming way when your partner is feeling good and can self-analyze with an attitude of detached curiosity. Describe the behaviours you observe and then ask your partner to comment about his or her feelings. Likely your partner is frustrated with it too, but will become defensive if feeling attacked by you. Once it is on the table as an issue you both are concerned with, the conflict resolution model can be employed to find solutions. In this way you will be able to understand more of how your partner experiences his or her reality, and you will have moved from a "what are you going to do about it stance?" to a "what can we do about?" stance. Addressing this moodiness together will assuredly make you a stronger, closer couple.

THE DOMINEERING PARTNER

Some of us have grown up to believe that if we are going to get what we want, we have to be in a position of power and control over others. Listen to the words of a couple who have spent a lot of time painfully working through their personality dynamics to establish a relationship of love. He says, "Helen, through marriage enrichment I've learned that I don't have to dominate you to get my needs met." She says, "Harold, I learned that I don't have to be devious to get what I want." This couple, well into their fifties, had likely spent many years in a dance of dominance and deviousness, attempting to get the love they wanted, but likely falling short, mainly because their approach was all wrong. Dominance usually alienates the affections of those on the receiving end. Dominance is different than leadership. Dominance has a bossy quality to it. Leadership encourages the contributions of others; dominance cuts them off. Domineering spouses often take rigid, unilateral positions. "We'll do it this way or not at all." "I'm not going, and that's final." Dominant partners often have difficulty listening to the views of others. The tragedy is that dominant people tend to kill the thing they love.

Dominant partners often have difficulty listening to the views of others. Like most of us, they value closeness, but behind their aggressive manner, is a great fear of being vulnerable.

If they were to let go of their controlling stance, they might risk being hurt. Thus they stick with the safety of dominance, a strategy doomed to fail. The tendency in dealing with domineering partners is to placate them and find ways around them. This is what Helen referred to as her deviousness. Once this pattern of deviousness and dominance has begun, genuine intimacy is threatened. Keeping money in accounts unknown to your partner, and buying things and hiding them from your partner for fear of what they might say are examples of deviousness that might arise in response to dominance. If you feel dominated, it's important to raise this as a general relationship concern before you get into deviousness and resentment. Talk about the impact of your partner's behaviour on your feelings and ask them if this is what they intend to do. Address it as a general relationship problem, a threat to the closeness you both want. Confess your own temptation towards methods that are manipulative and devious. In this spirit of confession, your partner is more likely to take a serious look at changing their pattern of interaction. Help them to see what might be in it for them. Healthy companionship marriages are based on democracy, equal power, shared openly by partners committed to each other.

Realistic Expectations

MATE SELECTION

Mate selection is not magical. There are many women in this world that I could be suitably matched with! Don't feel guilty because you agree with this statement. Rather, feel saddened for the person who, as Miriam and Aaron Arond described in their book, *The First Year of Marriage*, believes that if only they rode the subway of New York long enough, one day the subway door would open, and there would stand "Mr. or Mrs. Right!" The problem with the unrealistic romantic belief that there is only *one* person you could be happily mated with, in this world of five billion, is that it suggests that a great relationship is based on external forces such as luck, magic or some form of spiritual destiny. Most people in good relationships know that it is not luck - it's commitment and effort. A good relationship's success is "95 % perspiration and 5% inspiration." Sadly, there are many people who believe in the myth of "Mr. or Mrs. Right" and yearn for this mythical figure to appear and meet all their needs. This fantasy may hold some partners back from making a complete commitment of themselves to their current relationship.

Sadly, many people believe in the myth of "Mr. or Mrs. Right" and yearn for this mythical figure to appear and meet all their needs.

A person who enters a relationship with this type of fantasy or relationship belief could become easily disillusioned, and prone to blame "bad luck" on choosing a partner that is "not right for me." A guiding question in intimate relationships should be instead, "How can we become right for each other?" Asking the question "How can we become right for each other?" suggests that there are practical actions each partner can take to modify their behaviour patterns to suit the needs of the relationship. What this means is that you are claiming what psychologists call "an internal locus of control." You are choosing to run your own life! Yes, there may be times when certain couples seem absolutely perfect for each other. Chances are, however, that these seemingly "perfect matches" will have their trials of adjustment too. And, even if they don't, and you think that your mate has to be "one-in-a-million," remember what the Chinese say: "If you are one in a million in China, there are 1,000 others just like you!"

DISILLUSIONMENT . . . THE DANGER OF DENIAL

"Our relationship is so good now. I can't believe we'll have any problems!" People who hold this relationship belief when marrying are likely in for a big surprise! Naivete can appear as sweet, romantic innocence but in reality it can be detrimental. Even today, with the information bombardment of newspapers and television, seemingly sensible couples, when first in love, may truly believe that they will have no problems. This naivete is not reserved for the simple or inexperienced. In fact, many counsellors and clergy will tell you that remarrying and senior couples can be smitten with this kind of relationship thinking. This naivete is based on a form of denial. When "in denial" about something it is almost impossible for our psyche to acknowledge that something logically or obviously true could apply to us. This is why denial is detrimental. When the denial is eventually smashed - disillusionment is the consequence. The disillusionment is not with the idea of romance or with the other person (although this is part of it), but the with one's own judging ability.

All couples in marriage will at some time encounter problems.

Anyone who spouts the statement "I think we will never have problems in our marriage!" may be overconfident and in their self-absorption with love be neglecting an important fundamental of relationship life. Relationships change and move through many developmental phases. Each phase of life will bring new challenges. It is impossible to fully predict how anyone will fare. There are too many uncertainties to be totally confident. On the other hand, being too "problem-focused" is equally detrimental. Once it was thought that most couples going into marriage did so with a great deal of romantic naivete. Today, many couples enter marriage with a cynical or jaundiced view: a kind of resignation that it isn't likely to be helpful. The popular press and current folklore encourages this kind of negative view of marriage. Some trends in marriage therapy may lead us to a hopeful, more balanced view. Known as "solution focused" therapy, the emphasis is more on how to untangle knots than knowing how the knots got there, or who tied them. This is a view which greets problems as opportunities for growth in creative partnership. All couples in marriage will at some time encounter problems. The attitude one takes towards problems may determine whether the problems solidify and enhance the love in the relationship or destroy it!

"TIME HEALS ALL (OH REALLY?)"

ome people think that if you have a problem the best thing to do is just wait it out - ignore it, deny it, *anything* but confront it! These are people who subscribe to the theory that discussing problems will only lead to more hurts and frustrations. They may even point to some couples they knew who were always bringing their conflicts out in the open - who eventually wound up in divorce. "Better to let it go, to wait it out!" Is it? Consider what happens when relationship partners expect time to heal the inevitable injuries of intimate relations. Small irritations begin to add up to larger injuries. These injuries add up to resentments, which in turn, add up to deadened feelings. Rather than let the sparks fly, these "avoiders" allow the cinders to smoulder until they extinguish. To paraphrase the Dan Folgelberg song *Longer*, once love has died it is not easily exhumed.

**Sometimes the "time" you really need is the time to take
the courage to face the differences in your relationship.**

I once knew a young couple planning for their marriage. They had been dating for six years. They had many disagreements and conflicts, but they had taken the approach that, "Time would heal." They had not had the courage to face the implications of their differences. Their relationship became increasingly shallow through the years so that as the day of their wedding approached they had very little in common to speak about that was "safe." This led to depressed enthusiasm about the relationship and ambivalence about the approaching marriage. The dilemma of this couple is similar to living in a house and closing off rooms every time there is a disagreement about how to use or decorate that room. Eventually, all the rooms of the house come to be closed and all that is left to live in is the confining space of the hallways. In contrast, those relationship partners who confront problems relate that a new energy emerges. At times it may be painful, but most real growth is. There are certain relationship skills that need to be learned to enable problem-solving to be constructive. What's important here is to know that not confronting problems is a slow death by neglect for a love relationship. The mistaken notion that "Time Heals All" problems in relationships really covers up the fact that often there is a lack of courage to strive for something better in relationships. Think of something that has been bothering you in a relationship that you have been "letting slide" or hoping would disappear with time. Using your best social skills, confront the issue with the person involved and see if it does not add a new dimension or validity to that relationship.

19

TIME COMMITMENT

If we had more time together, our relationship would be better!" Many couples in our fast-paced style of life bemoan the lack of time to do things together as a couple. Often they think that if they only had more time together, their relationship would automatically improve. Consider the case of Jody and John. They have a busy schedule and a three year old son. Frequently they have fights which leave them wondering about the value of trying to make the relationships work. Jody, in particular, thinks that if they had more time together they would be much happier. Jody may be right. For many couples in the early child-rearing stage, there are an incredible number of duties and strains with little time left over for doing "couple things" that might enhance the relationship. In fact, if you are in this stage of life it may be important for you to put your experience into a broader framework. These are likely the most limiting years of married life and usually the years of lowest marital satisfaction. So don't despair; it often gets better.

**Time commitment may be what your relationship needs;
on the other hand "time" is only part of the formula.**

However, more time together may not cure all of the problems of Jody and John's relationship. In fact, more time together may just remind them of how little they really understand or suit each other. There are times when couples choose to be apart as a means of stabilizing a relationship that isn't working. These are often couples who are so preoccupied with external sources that they never have to confront what is lacking within their relationship. Emptiness can be masked by busyness. There are times when couples take a holiday as a means of reviving a relationship. Holidays can be a healing tonic, but if there are underlying inequities, misunderstandings and long-standing resentments, they will likely still be there when the holiday is over. There are many couples who have little time together but who recognize this as a necessary part of the kind of lifestyle they have chosen. These couples will strive to make the time they *do* have for each other into quality times. When they are able to connect, the meeting is enriching and pleasurable. For others, however, their time together is stilted or filled with distractions. They talk about "safe" functional topics that fail to connect them at any depth. Taking time for relationships is important. But time of itself will not build a meaningful relationship. Time + vulnerability + confronting problems + playfulness is more likely to be the formula you need to get the relationship you want!

Intimate Relationships Can't Be Everything

T here are times when love provides the feeling that there is need for no one else to complete one's joy. Whether it is a couple in the early stages of romance or a family that has just set off on a well-deserved holiday, there are moments in life when we feel a euphoria about relationships that says "There is nothing more that is necessary!" This is a wonderful feeling that should be treasured, but not possessed. Why? Because attempts to control and confine this feeling lead to stagnant, jealous relationships. Imagine that you are newly married. You have been away on a great honeymoon where you felt a wonderful closeness. You ate, slept, toured and spent literally every waking moment of the day with your partner. You get home and immediately want to call up a friend to share some of your excitement . . . your partner looks a bit uptight but neither one of you says a thing. Over time, when you join something new, go for lunch with a friend or simply talk on the phone, your partner looks dejected.

**Healthy relationship partners know that they
can't satisfy all of their partner's needs.**

What is happening is the making of a jealous, possessive relationship when one party thinks that this relationship should meet all his or her needs for security, support and companionship. This irrational relationship belief is what fuels many battles in marriages and families! The solution to this issue is permeability of boundaries. Think of a family or a relationship being like a primary living cell. If the membrane encompassing the cell is too tight, no new elements can be absorbed. The cell must live within itself. Without new sources of nourishment from the outside, the cell will eventually deteriorate and die. If the cell membrane is too permeable the cell is vulnerable and susceptible to disintegration. The boundary requires permeability so that new elements can be incorporated, but has enough definition to defy disintegration. Expecting that an intimate relationship will satisfy all of one's needs for companionship and security leads to a unhealthy restriction - a kind of relationship self-centredness. At worst, it leads to bizarre relationships where each partner is captive to the other. Healthy relationship partners know that they cannot satisfy all of their partner's needs. They welcome the chance for both themselves and their loved one to interact with others in a way that provides depth and growth to their relationship!

THE MYTH OF UNSHAKABLE LOVE

W ho would have thought that the Berlin Wall would ever come down, or that we would see statues replaced in Red Square? Who would have thought that Jimmy Swaggart would be caught in sexual indiscretions, not once, but twice?! Certainly the world needs heroes and leaders, but given the track record, very few would want to be put on a pedestal. Lovers or relationships should not be either! There are certain kinds of personality styles most prone to accepting the "Myth of Unshakable Love." People with a strong dose of mercurial personality style, the healthy variant of the borderline personality disorder, are apt to think that nothing could change their present feelings for someone they love. They cannot conceive that at some point they might be disappointed, resentful, or even downright hateful towards their relationship partner. People who have a strong dose of the "dramatic" personality style also tend to confer a sense of eternity or "this is forever" on their present feeling state.

**Realistic relationship partners know that each member
of the relationship is made of clay, changing as they move
through the various developmental stages of life.**

Unfortunately, the more strongly one tends to believe the myth of unshakable love, the harder one is apt to fall when disappointed. This is especially so for many second-married persons who thought they had learned it all in the first relationship and were so certain it could not go wrong the second time around. Once again they were blind to small flaws which, over time, became big cracks in the relationship. Realistic relationship partners know that each member of the relationship is made of clay. People change as they move through the various developmental stages of life. People make mistakes. Love moves through phases of closeness and distance and relationships hold a differential attraction at different times. These are facts that can sustain people in relationships over the long haul. Knowing these facts means that love does not have to be passionate and intense at all times in order to be valued. Euphoric love is not put on a pedestal above other kinds of love. A love that is thought to be unshakable is likely built on a very flimsy foundation. Mature relationship partners seek to understand the frailty in their relationship and take preventative steps through courses or counselling to realistically appraise the relationship so that negative surprises are minimized. It is a tragedy that many enlightened couples marry without using the fine marriage preparation resources available today. Unfortunately, unlike the Berlin Wall, the "Myth of Unshakable Love" still remains with us!

WHY WON'T YOU CHANGE

As irrational as it may sound, many people have married with the belief that they would be able to change their partner *after* they were married! This is typical thinking of the so-called "co-dependent" person who marries someone because they believe that eventually, with the proper kind of caretaking, their partner will change. He'll give up drinking; he'll give up womanizing; he'll settle down. Notice the negative examples are male. That is because women are more apt to identify this "marrying of potential" syndrome. I've known several brides-to-be who said that their partner would not attend a marriage preparation program, even though the bride wanted to. Such a program might help them learn effective communication skills and lay a solid basis for the marriage. I've told them frankly "If he won't seek help with you now, it's less likely that he ever will, even if you have serious problems." These brides are examples of people who have wishful thinking about changing their partners. According to family theorists, however, most of us marry with the hope of changing our partner.

> **According to family theorists most of us marry with the hope of changing our partner. We seek what is comfortable and so attempt to engineer our partner into patterns and roles familiar from our family of origin.**

We seek what is comfortable and so attempt to engineer our partner into patterns and roles familiar from our own family of origin. It is as if we find a partner and say, "Let's play house . . . here is your role and this is how I would like it to go!". The complicating factor is that each person in the dyad hopes to be the director of the play. Each is casting the other for the lead part. Thus the theory goes that even if we are not aware of wanting to change our partners, in a myriad of minor ways we attempt to have them fulfil the childhood picture images we have of our first loved objects, usually our parents. Realistic relationships partners know that they may be able to influence their partner, but that they cannot make their partner change. Indeed, the more one pushes for change, the more resistance to change they may create in their partner, thus sabotaging the very thing they hope to achieve. Relationship partners wanting change need to be aware that change is a reciprocal process. One has to ask oneself, "What is it that my partner may want me to change that I would be willing to do?" The next step is to address change as something *you* want, not necessarily from the other person, but from the relationship. The more expectations are addressed openly, rationally and sensitively, the more likely it is you will influence your partner. But don't expect your partner to change. Expect changes in the dynamics of your relationship as a play of a give and take by both of you!

THE FALLACY OF BELIEVING YOU REALLY KNOW SOMEONE

One of the deadliest of all relationship beliefs is that you can reach a point when you know all there is to know about your partner. What could be more boring than to spend the rest of your life with someone you know everything about? Where is the mystery, the joy of discovery, the growth? Based on the fallacy that they really know one another, some couples break up hoping to find someone who is new and interesting. Usually this represents either a running away from knowing oneself or a mistaken belief that intimacy comes easily. In reality, if you are in an intimate relationship and you think that you know all there is to know about your partner, you are likely being naive. First of all, it's a job just to know yourself, let alone share that knowledge with someone else. Secondly, human beings are constantly changing and developing as they move through their lives. Hence their perceptions, their opinions and their feelings change.

> **In reality, if you are in an intimate relationship and you think that you know all there is to know about your partner, you're likely being naive.**

A young woman who married when she was a passive and insecure nineteen year old, may be quite a different person at twenty-nine. By that point she may have graduated from college, had a few children and grown immensely in self-assurance. A man who as a young husband was self-centred with little interest in emotional intimacy with his wife, may at age 35, be ready for non-sexual closeness. The inevitable losses and deepening experiences of life change us all. At times our compulsions and dysfunctions grow and have greater reign. At other times we find the grace to overcome long-standing imperfections and grow in positive, relationship-nurturing ways. The point is, that change is an inevitable part of human development. People in exciting marriages cultivate the expectation that they are never the same person they were yesterday . . . not exactly anyway. Certainly there must be comfort and consistency in relationships, but that there is always something new should not be overlooked. Assuming change in others is a helpful way to anticipate and adapt to change in yourself. This perspective makes life more of an adventure. To be in an intimate relationship is to have a box seat on the drama of lives unfolding. Intimate relationships provide us the privilege of being the audience as well as the actor!

MARRIAGE: THE PLACE OF DIMINISHING OR DEEPENING LOVE

Most marriages are languishing for limited romantic love. Whenever I speak to groups about marriage, I ask the group what percentage of the married population do they believe has truly romantic marriages. The highest estimates are 20%. The usual is 5%. This is a real tragedy, since romantic love is so often what brings people together and seems to make relationships exciting. If one wants to be realistic about relationships, then one would expect that romantic love would begin to wilt as time goes by. But does it have to? Or is this assumed fact about relationships really a self-fulfilling prophecy . . . we expect romance to diminish and so it does. What would happen if we knew that romance in relationships would change and likely fade but that it could make way for new kinds of romance within the relationship? That seems to be the attitude of couples who take marriage enrichment courses.

In long-term relationships, involuntary "out of control" romantic love will definitely fade but it can be replaced by a more voluntary, deliberate romantic love.

The first romantic love comes easily, involuntarily. Usually people don't have a sense that they are doing anything to make it happen. It feels like something that happens to them. We say that we "fall in love," giving the picture of being out of control. Certainly in long term relationships this involuntary "out of control" romantic love will definitely fade. It can be replaced, however, by a more voluntary, deliberate romantic love. This is where romance becomes a choice. Here we chose to think the best of our partner, to look for the best in them, to speak the best about them and to treat them as if they were the best. In other words, it's something that is cultivated. Let's add to this the experience of people in the marriage enrichment movement who say that a growing marriage is like serial monogamy. If you actively acknowledge the changes through developmental experiences at each stage, it can be like getting a brand new husband or wife. Various crises of life can also add a sense of being in a new relationship. If one is sensitive to these changes, one can see that there will be new opportunities for romance. At one point in the relationship, flowers or chocolates may have been romantic. At another point, volunteering to look after the kids and house while your mate goes out with a friend may be what really counts. Consequently life provides new material from which romance can spring. Does romance fade in marriage? Usually. Does romance have to fade in marriage? Not necessarily. Romantic love can go from a whirlwind force beyond our control to deepening love well within our command. The key is in appreciating the changes of life and making a conscious choice to keep those love fires burning.

RELATIONSHIP PROBLEMS: PRE AND POST MARRIAGE

Few people today would agree with the idea that problems that exist before marriage will somehow magically dissolve once they marry. Only a die hard few believe that people marry and live happily ever after . . . that is, of course, when you speak to them rationally about someone else's relationship. It isn't so easy to see this truth when applied to oneself. Instead it's easy to believe that the future will wash out any problems that the couple may experience. Think of this couple I once knew who were to be married for the second time. They had a number of communication problems, particularly when it came to the discipline of her kids. They attributed much of the problem to the fact that the man worked in a town 60 miles away and only came home on weekends. When they married, the family was to move to his town. This couple glossed over their communication and parenting differences assuming it was the lack of stability in the living arrangements, the constant coming and going that was adding pressure which was leading to problems.

Most qualified marriage counsellors can likely find the seeds of a relationship's destruction in the premarital experience of that couple. Research has shown that communication patterns at the premarital stage are predictive of relationship problems post marriage.

In fact, this couple found that when they moved together, their communication problem and parenting differences became all the more evident. Their previous living arrangement had shielded them from the scope of the problem. Faced with it every day, they both quickly despaired for the marriage. The experience of this couple is typical of relationship problems. They don't just fade away; they tend to expand. In fact, most qualified marriage counsellors can likely find the seeds of a relationship's destruction (whether this be through divorce or simply a loss of love) in the premarital experience of that couple. Research has shown that communication patterns at the premarital stage are predictive of relationship problems post marriage. Issues in one's family of origin stand out like red flags on a football field, yet the relationship partners may be oblivious to them. Often there are hurts and resentments that develop during courtship that continue to damage the quality of relationship experience. Weddings themselves are often times fraught with potential for hurt feelings. No one would expect that a car with a leaking radiator would fix itself. The problem is only going to get worse. The same is usually true in relationships. It's always better to confront relationship problems at their root, early in their development. Usually at that point there are enough positives to carry the relationship through to resolutions of the issues.

Communication

ACCURATE COMMUNICATION:
THE CORE OF COMPANIONSHIP

R obert Fulgum has written a popular book which speaks a great truth in its title, *All I Need to Know I Learned in Kindergarten*. As the philosophers say - the opposite of a great truth is another great truth. In this case, even the best lessons of kindergarten usually have not prepared relationship partners with the skills they will need to get the love they want or to be the kind of partner they set out to be. Good intentions are not enough. A high school education is not enough. Usually a university degree will not make the difference either. What is usually required is some specialized training in the skills of communication. At this point you might protest, "Have not people been communicating for years? Haven't relationships survived without specialized communication training?" The answer, of course, is that people have communicated for years. In fact, it is impossible for people not to communicate. Everything we do communicates something. Even silence can speak volumes! And yes, there are people who are specially gifted with the ability to speak and listen, but they often stand out as exceptions, more than the rule. What makes our kindergarten skills inadequate for relationships today are changed expectations. Today we expect that a good relationship will naturally bring to us deep, interpersonal communication. More is demanded of relationships today and thus effective communication skills are required.

Everything we do communicates something.
Even silence can speak volumes.

Good communication in this new context means having the ability to attend to the most minute stirrings of the psyche, both our own and our partner's. At one time a great communicator was someone who could get their ideas across to others in a kind of sales-pitch. This created great preachers, politicians and polemicists, but not great partners. Good relationships have an equality where information of similar importance is reciprocated between partners. The "silver-tongued" oracle usually communicates only in one direction. The ultimate desire today in relationships is for companionship. Companionship thrives on revelations of the heart. Within a relationship of trust, each partner finds the safety to explore his or her own inner world. The skills required to do this are similar to those learned by trained counsellors. Counsellors learn that often we have difficulty communicating what we really mean. Often it takes two people to discover the unique meanings of the one. In my practice of marriage therapy, I have found that most couples can learn the skills they need to do this. If they are learning while in crises, it may take longer. If they are learning at a time when their relationship is good, it may take as little as twelve hours, a small investment indeed for an asset so important to the success of a relationship!

"THE FIRST HALF OF COMMUNICATION: SPEAKING FOR SELF"

C ommunication can be broken down into two major skill areas, speaking and listening. Good communicators within intimate relationships have to do both well. They can listen sensitively to their partner and they can accurately portray their own experience in ways that are understandable to others. At the outset it might seem a simple thing to speak for one's "self," but, in fact, very few people do it well. This is because speaking for self means more than being able to spout a lot of words; it means really knowing oneself. The first attribute, then, of an effective communicator is courage. It takes courage to take the journey inward, to become a student of one's own soul and psyche, to lay vulnerable one's needs, wants and desires. It is here one can learn to appreciate feelings of ambivalence and anxiety. Those with the courage to study the undercurrents of their emotional lives develop a certain distance from themselves which allows some measure of detachment or objectivity. This state of detachment will prove immeasurably helpful in relationship discussions. It allows relationship partners to talk about their needs without impassioned rhetoric, without anger or abuse or other methods of coercion and control.

When you have taken time to know yourself, then you move into the phase of dialogue with your partner.

When I present week-end seminars for couples, one of the first communication exercises assigned is for each partner to take time to write down his or her thoughts, feelings and wants in relation to any issue in their relationship. The analogy is drawn between this and the standard sex therapy treatment for orgasmic dysfunction. In sex therapy, one is encouraged to begin by learning about one's own body and what gives it pleasure. This phase of therapy is completed alone. Not until we know about ourselves sexually can we begin to speak to our partner about what is pleasing. The same is true of all aspects of intimate relationships. When you have taken time to know yourself, then you move into the phase of "dialogue" with your partner. Speaking for your "self" also implies that you are conscious of the other voices that may be carried around in your head. There is the voice of your conscience - the "should and ought centre" of your brain. There is the voice of your mother and father or other significant figures in your life. There may also be a voice within that is the rebel self which is merely the shadow opposite of various voices of authority. A person who can speak for him or her "self" knows all of these parts and can discern among them an authentic or personal "self." Thus when you speak for yourself, you do not say what your mother would want you to say, or what you think a "real man" or a "good girl" ought to say. You represent only your true "self." Anyone entering a serious relationship is cautioned to take time to know this true self, for it is only when you know yourself, that you can truly speak for your "self."

"SELF" CENTRED SPEAKING

W hen you were small, it was likely that your parents encouraged you not to be self-centred. In contrast, in relationship training it is important that each partner learn to speak in a way that is "self" centred, that is, to speak in a way that reveals your true "self." "Self" centred speaking usually begins with the pronoun, "I." Observe, if you will, a couple having a fight. You are likely to hear a lot of "you" centred language. "You never live up to your commitments, do you?" she accused. "Well, who'd want to do that for you anyway?" he retorts. Notice, neither of them used the pronoun "I." Their speech was full of blame, with no one speaking for themselves. What is it that these marital partners might be feeling? No one really knows, because neither spoke for his or her "self." If the couple in our example was to speak for themselves individually, you might expect them to say something like the following: "I feel hurt, as if I'm not important enough to be considered!" she comments. "I know I haven't been that thoughtful; I feel guilty about that and don't know how to make it better," he might say. Notice that there is no longer any blame. Each partner is speaking for him or herself. "You" messages frequently lead to blaming and alienation. "I" messages can break down the pattern of mutual blame, helping relationship partners to understand what role they can play in improving the relationship.

**Think of something you would like to change in a relationship
with someone else and have a conversation with them
without once using the pronoun "you."**

It is easy to give "you" messages. However it is not so easy to focus on or discern the feelings behind the personage that you call "I." Try this exercise. Think of something you would like to change in a relationship with someone else and have a conversation with him or her without once using the pronoun "you." It would be all right to say words such as "our relationship" and this is how "I feel," but not the word "you." You'll be amazed how hard it is to focus on what it is that you think, feel and want, without straying over into accusations and attributions about that person. Although it is always good to consider the needs of your partner, the pronoun "you," should be seldom heard when intimates are discussing issues or conflicts close to the heart. What is more helpful is to let your partner know who the feeling "you" really is through "I" statements that are thoughtful revelations of your inner most being.

EXPRESSING ALL THE PARTS OF YOUR "SELF"

Every human notion is made up of personal experiences, thoughts, feelings and wishes. Some of us are primarily cognitive; we feel most comfortable when we are talking about what we think. Others of us are very emotional. We know what we feel without having to have a reason for feeling that way. Whichever our area of strength, we are apt to neglect some part of our experience when attempting to communicate our true "self" to our partner. The *Couple Communication Program* developed by Miller, Nunnally and Wackman offers a simple formula for ensuring that you reveal all the parts of your "self" within intimate relationships. First, begin with an "I" statement, rather than a "you" statement. Then report what in particular you sense, what you think, what you feel and what you want... "I sense... I think... I feel... I want." It's a simple formula that packs a lot of potential for powerful communication. When you hear people using this model, you might hear them beginning with something like "What I'm hearing" or, "The way I see it...." In this way the speaker is reporting his or her sensory data. This data cannot be challenged. The way you see it, the way your hear it, the way you smell it, the way it tastes to you, the way it touches you, is all something that only you can report on.

Looking for a more intimate relationship with your partner?
Try this formula: "I sense, I think, I feel, I want"

Different people experience differently. This might not seem profound, but in marriages, remembering this simple truth can eliminate a lot of fights. Once you can report on what your senses take in, you need to tell your partner what you think about it. If you see a wrinkled brow, you might think that means "worried." Next, you can report how you feel. You might feel concerned and want to help. All of this says much more than, "What's the matter?" From "What's the matter?" one might infer concern but it isn't as direct as the "I" message. Marital partners are often concerned that their loved one might cheat on them. I would like to give you a new definition of what it means to "cheat" on your partner. It means to give your partner less than you have promised. It means to hold back on sharing parts of your self. Some "cheat" by never telling how they really feel and by not taking the time to find out. Others are afraid to state what they really want and so their loved ones have to guess. Some keep their thinking and the experiences it is based on, (their senses), a secret. This is also what cheating is about. Using this simple formula from the *Couple Communication Program*, I sense, I think, I feel, I want, it is possible to reveal valuable information that can lead to greater mutual understanding and to that ultimate goal of relationships - intimacy.

31

THE HEART OF THE MATTER

Expressing emotions may not be difficult; expressing them accurately is. When you make an attempt to reveal yourself to your partner it is important to accurately process your emotions. This "process" means to identify those emotions that a particular situation evokes within you and then report them in a way that makes sense to your listener. Getting mad and yelling accusations certainly will let people know that you are expressing negative emotions. It will not, however, help them to understand that you might also have felt hurt, rejected or lonely. Yet very likely these are the emotions that lie beneath the surface of your anger and rage. You might think of emotions as coming in two major varieties. The first, called secondary emotions, usually create distance between people. Rage is a perfect example. It is hard to feel close to someone who is raging at you. Rage usually engenders feelings of counter rage. Soon, you have two angry people. The other major variety of emotions are primary. These are basic, the closest to our beings core. These often lie under the secondary emotions. For example, in a situation where you feel furious about something, when you stop to think about it you will likely find that underscoring this secondary emotion are the primary emotions of fear or hurt. An angry person usually means a hurt person.

Think what would happen if every time you became angry you could process your anger and understand the hurt beneath.

Instead of raging at your partner, you share the hurt or fear that you feel. Sharing the hurt will likely be less threatening to your partner. This softer approach is more apt to focus attention on you and towards a solution to your hurt, whereas the secondary emotion of anger would create defensiveness and lead to counter blame. When processing emotions, it is important to remember that human emotions are complex. Depending on the circumstances, you might feel a variety of emotions in response to the same stimulus. You might have feelings about your feelings. You might feel shame about your rage or jealousy. You might feel guilty about feeling sexually attracted to someone other than your partner. You might feel rejected, but silly, for feeling so insecure. Processing emotions means working through and understanding this complex web. Try this little exercise. Next time you feel angry, frustrated, furious or annoyed with your partner, think the experience through. Is there a softer emotion, like feeling lonely, abandoned, or defeated that you could share with your partner instead of anger. Approach with the softer feeling and see what happens!

FEELING EMOTIONS, THINKING THOUGHTS

In an effort to communicate how they really feel, many relationship partners mistakenly talk about what they think, instead of what they feel. Consider this couple who are talking about their financial situation. He says, "I feel we should put as much into saving for a house as we possibly can and spend money on holidays once we have a house paid for." Substitute the words "think" for "feel" in his statement. It is more accurate because what he has expressed is really more what he thinks, not what he feels. If he were telling what he feels, he would be using words that describe his emotions. Instead he might say, "I'm feeling insecure (an emotional word) about our finances and I worry (another emotional word) about this so much, it's hard for me to enjoy holidays." In this statement he has provided some of the emotional background for understanding his thinking processes. There is a tremendous interaction between what we think and what we fee. It's hard to understand how people think in relationships unless you understand something of how they feel. Thus using the common idiom of speech "I feel" and then describing mental processes instead of feelings, can lead to a lot of misunderstandings. Just because your partner has said the words "I feel," does not mean that he or she has really told you what is felt.

Confusing "I feel" with "I think," can lead to a lot of misunderstanding.

What would happen if the husband who wanted to put more money into savings failed to tell his wife about his insecurity and worry? If she thought they should spend some money now and enjoy life because she was feeling restless, she would likely be feeling frustrated with him. She might conclude that he is a stick-in-the-mud who is attempting to control her and doom her to a life of "all work and no play." If she heard about his feelings, his worry and insecurity, she could likely relate. Feelings have a way of being universal. Although she may not worry about the same things, she can understand the paralysis the feeling of insecurity brings. This will help her to be more sensitive when discussing and working through this issue. Using the same example, unless she clearly told her husband about her feelings of trapped restlessness, he may mistakenly think that she is being an insensitive spendthrift. Together they can resolve her restless feeling and his insecure feelings in a way which can meet both of their needs. But this cannot happen if they are unable to distinguish a thought from a feeling. For the rest of this day, monitor your own speech patterns or that of others. Do the words "I feel" preface thoughts or emotions? You will soon notice how to differentiate!

LISTENING LOVE

Howard Clinebell, pastoral counsellor and author, has called the kind of "message receiving" used by therapists *listening love.* By this, Clinebell meant that the therapist provides an open ear that is trained to listen to the most intimate expressions of individuality, pain and joy. Clients would express that this kind of attentive listening from their therapist is a form of freeing love that provides a safe place for them to explore and know themselves at a deeper level. Since the early days of the counselling movement, counsellors have recognized that many of these same listening skills can be taught to all people for the enrichment of their relationships. The primary skills of listening in relationships are presented in the *Couple Communication Program.* They consist of attending to your partner, tracking verbal and non-verbal expressions, and providing feedback on what you are hearing. The guiding principle is that each partner is focused on the exploration and expression of the other. This type of "other centred" communication differs from every day "coffee shop" kind of exchanges.

> **Using the *listening love* model can help you get past**
> **emotional facades to the more primary feelings**
> **upon which relationships can be built.**

In everyday communication, people give and receive messages or information exchanges, often without checking to see if the message sent was received and understood. One person makes a comment, giving their views. The other responds in kind, sharing what they think about the matter at hand. This can easily lead to the situation of two people talking perfunctorily with nobody really listening. I like to compare marriages where there are fights and contentious issues to tennis matches with both people serving at the same time. The *listening love* model slows this process down, so that people begin to pay attention to what the first speaker says. The second speaker does not reply with his or her own thoughts until they are clear they understand what was said. Consequently, there can be a lot of cross-checking until it is determined that the message sent was the message received. Taking the matter further, they might want to be clear that the message received was not only what was sent, but what was intended. Sometimes people say things in anger, when what they really mean to convey is that they are lonely and don't know what to do about it. A person using the *listening love* model would be able to get past the angry facade to the more primary feelings upon which the relationship can be built. The model is called *listening love* because the listener has to put himself aside and focus his attention on truly understanding their partner. When people listen to what we have to say, we feel valued, we feel loved.

ATTENDING

T he first of the listening skills taught to couples who want to break cycles of destructive communication is so simple, it will seem self-evident. The skill is paying attention to one's partner. It is amazing how many ways there are to communicate non-attention. First, you can look impatient or bored when your partner is trying to communicate something complex. Likely you have not scheduled the time to spend hearing what your partner has to say, and your body language shows it. Impatience is indicated by rolling the eyes, yawning or fidgeting. Or, you can do what many non-attenders do - "pretend" to listen when they are mentally adrift, thinking about something else. If you want to be really nonattentive you can turn the radio to a different station while your partner is talking, find a new page in the paper to glance at, or keep one eye on the hockey game on the television. A particularly annoying effect is created by cleaning your finger nails while your partner speaks, or, if you like a little paradoxical message for fun, you can pick lint off your partner's sweater or attempt to straighten his tie while they are trying to tell you something important. Then, if they accuse you of not listening, you can protest that you were only trying to help. Slouching in a chair is another sure fire way to discourage a speaker, or to heighten their anxiety and sense of alienation, cross you legs and fold your arms on your chest. Then say, "So talk, you wanted to talk!"

How well do you "attend?"
One way to find out is to let your partner rate you.

People who attend well do several things and none of the things mentioned above. This is what they do. They orient their bodies to suggest that they want to listen. This usually means eye contact. They position their bodies in such a way that their body posture suggests openness and alertness. They make sure that they have a psychological readiness. If they are not feeling ready to listen, they will ask to postpone the conversation until later. This doesn't mean stalling or avoidance; it means booking a time when they really think they are able to set aside enough time to truly hear what is being said. Genuine attending is the first step in the process of letting your partner know that you care enough to put aside your own needs and speeches, to focus on him or her. A good way to determine your attending skills is to ask your partner and then to listen - with attention!

TRACKING YOUR PARTNER

How do you get to think the way you do?" "What was happening that lead to the way you feel?" These are the kinds of questions that you want answers to when you are genuinely interested in listening to your partner. The skill you are demonstrating is called "*tracking*." There are a number of specific techniques you will want to use when tracking your partner in conversation, but first it is important to get a sense of the purpose of this skill. It is not unlike tracking someone in the bush. You follow the speaker's trail of conversation. What you take note of are key or guiding words and non-verbal expressions. The purpose is to determine what they are trying to convey and how they got there. This can be put in the form of a question, "What's it like to be you?" In order to understand the unique experience of your partner, you will need to use one of a variety of skills. If your partner is a fairly verbal, articulate person, all he or she will need is your attention. As he or she talks, you can give them little "encouragers" that let them know you are tracking. Expressions like "I see," "I'm with you," "um hum" are ways of letting your partner know that you're on board with their thoughts.

Not only do you need to find the right clues to enable you to track your partner's words and non-verbal expressions but you have to let them know you are on track once you do.

If your partner is the quiet type, or if he or she often has difficulty putting in words what is really close to the heart, then you might need some of the other tracking skills. One such skill is silence. Give your partner time to find the words they need. Highly verbal speakers often find it difficult to listen to a partner who has a slower, more thoughtful kind of response. This can lead to the annoying habit of interjecting and "talking for" a partner. This of course leads to even more reticence to speak on the part of the more silent partner. Questions are also important in tracking. But a word of caution ... use questions that are open-ended that do not invite a simple "yes" or "no" response. Avoid asking questions that begin with the word "why," since this usually provokes rationalization, and a lot of our intimate experience is non-rational. Finally, there are the "door openers." These are expressions such as "Tell me more," or "Keep on," or "Help me understand." Don't be too specific in your request, just try to prompt your partner to open up. Appropriate use of encouragers, door openers, questions and silence can play an important part, helping you to understand your mate. Essential behind these techniques is a sincere desire on your part to understand your partner as an interesting and unique human being. This kind of genuine interest is bound to be reciprocated in how your partner feels about you and the relationship between you!

FEEDBACK

H ere are two words that you should avoid saying to your partner - "*I understand.*" In reality we can *attempt* to understand, we can **want** to understand, but in the long run, what really matters is that your partner believes that you understand. Saying, "I understand," does not prove anything. Unfortunately these words are often used glibly or to interrupt someone else's train of thought. "All right, lay off, I understand!" Have you ever heard that before? Announcing understanding with relationships should be the prerogative of the one who is sending the message. If a husband is trying to figure out what his partner is saying, he'll use the last of the three major listening skills, known as *feedback,* to demonstrate his understanding. When this is done, then his wife can conclude, "Yes, I think you do understand." This conclusion should be left to the one who has been doing the speaking, not to the one doing the listening. Giving feedback can be a difficult skill to master. Many people tell me they find it unnatural at first. They are more used to speaking and not taking the time to be sure they understood what the other person had to say. Giving feedback does just that - the conversation does not go any further until you have clarified what the first speaker has said.

The important thing here is that you make sure you know what your partner has said, and more importantly, what they meant, before you respond to them with your thoughts and feelings.

Feedback can be divided into three general levels. Level one is known as *parroting* or "word-for-word" feedback. When people are giving feedback you will hear them saying things like "So, I hear you saying . . . ?" or "Are you saying . . . ?" There is a tentative tone, always respecting the fact that you may not be relating exactly what they mean for you to hear. Parroting can be a helpful skill, particularly when people have developed a habit of not taking the time to process what their partner said before speaking themselves. *Paraphrasing* is a way to summarize what your partner has told you. What is important here is to ensure that you feedback the feelings and the main points, without reducing the message of your partner so that it seems trivial or insignificant. A more challenging level of feedback is *empathy.* Empathy has often been described as "walking in the other person's shoes." This involves feedback of not only what your partner said with words, but what was said between the lines. Since this involves a greater level of inference, it is even more important that empathic feedback be done in a carefully respective manner. The important thing is that you make sure you know what your partner has said and more importantly, what they <u>meant</u>, before you respond to them with your thoughts and feelings. If you want to improve your marriage by enhancing your communication, it may be time to ask an in-house expert about your use of communication skills - your partner!

Conflict
Resolution

GIVING UP

T here is a joke about women in the workplace, a joke which is told at the expense of men. This joke reveals hostility based on the way women are often treated in our society, that is, "one down." In this joke, it's the men who are put "one down." It goes like this: " In order for a woman to succeed in business she has to be twice as smart as a man. Fortunately, this isn't difficult!" As we move towards a society liberated from limiting stereotypes, it gets harder to determine what really are true sex differences and what are simply cultural biases. One genuine sex difference, according to Dr. John Gottman of Seattle, is the differential physiological response of men and women to marital conflict. In his marital interaction research lab, Dr. Gottman has measured certain vital signs, such as pulse and skin response, and found that anger arousal in a marital conflict takes far longer to dissipate in men than women. This means that women tend to get mad and get over it. The unpleasant side effects of conflict tend to linger on for the men.

**Giving up on conflict needs to be recognized
as a dangerous threat to any relationship.**

As a consequence, men are likely to find marital conflict to be much more unpleasant than do their wives. In response, men use a self-protective coping skill known as "stonewalling." Stonewalling, as it sounds, is a technique of acting like there is a stone wall between you and your partner. As such, it seems like the one who "stonewalls" has given up before he or she begins. It's important to understand the motivation behind stonewalling. Like the turtle going into its shell, the object is self-protection. To an outsider, the stonewalling partner may look defeated. They don't fight back; they just take it or they acquiesce. To the one who receives the stonewalling, this "quitting before we begin," feels like the gang who is left at the ballpark after the kid who owns the ball goes home in a huff. It seems like a bid to control the relationship unilaterally. It's important to realize that "giving up" on conflict does not help the relationship. It may settle things down in the short run but the long term prognosis is poor. Giving up usually leaves one party feeling victimized and the other feeling abandoned. Walking away from a marital conflict can be a valuable step when it is used as a "time out" to cool off before getting down to the serious work of solving problems. Giving up on conflict needs to be recognized as a dangerous threat to any relationship. If this "giving up too soon" pattern persists after efforts to change it, then relationship counselling is warranted.

DISAGREEING ABOUT DISAGREEING

T he story is told about the porcupines who needed to be warm on a cold winter night. They moved towards each other but when they got too close their quills inevitably hurt one another. So they moved apart. Once apart, they became aware of the cold and so moved toward each other in an effort to find warmth. This back and forth manoeuvring happened until they found just the right distance: close enough to feel each other's warmth, but far enough apart that their quills didn't hurt each other. Although sometimes used as a means to find intimacy, conflict in intimate relationships can be the means we use to establish distance when someone feels too close for comfort. In this way, conflict is merely understood as a mechanism for negotiating closeness and distance. Often this is done simply by arguing about arguing. There are times when couples fight about how they fight. One partner may be dramatic and emotional. When there is a disagreement, this person wants passion and intensity. Another may be super-reasonable and want lists and force field analysis, a careful accounting of who got what. This couple can sling mud such as, "You're always so cold and analytical" or "You're totally unreasonable!" You can see that this "arguing about arguing" can become very destructive.

Every couple needs to find a process that allows each partner to get the needed warmth from their relationship without hurting each other.

Certainly there are better ways to negotiate the amount of distance and closeness that each party to the relationship requires. Rather than getting bogged down in "arguing about arguing," it's important to understand why your partner handles conflict the way they do. Often, those who like to ventilate their feelings need the reassurance that they are loved. Without reciprocal displays of emotion from their partner, they may feel abandoned. The partner who favours "reasoning" may fear losing control if he or she allows themselves to experience emotions. It is important for each partner to respect the needs behind the "conflict style" of the other. Together they should agree on a process whereby "ventilating" becomes "expression of feelings," and "reasoning" becomes "co-operative problem-solving." A super-reasonable person would likely never be comfortable with ventilating feelings. They may be persuaded to describe and eventually express how they feel. Ventilators can learn to channel their emotions so that they seem less dramatic or threatening to a non-demonstrative partner. There may be no particular or specific "right way" to handle conflict. But every couple needs to find a process that allows each partner to get the needed warmth from their relationship without hurting each other. Finding this comfortable conflict style should be one of the first things serious relationship partners accomplish.

UNDERSTANDING IS GREATER THAN AGREEMENT

O ne of the greatest obstacles to the resolution of marital conflict is that partners often fail to listen to each other. They may have heard a lot but without really understanding what the other has been trying to say. Unfortunately we often have built-in prejudices about truly understanding people. One such prejudice is the unrealistic relationship belief that to understand someone implies that you agree with them. This is not how it should work in intimate relationships! Understanding should be a starting point on the path towards an agreed solution, but understanding should never imply agreement. It is this fear - if I really listen to you and understand your point of view, then I will have to agree with you - that blocks our hearing. Often what occurs in marital disagreements is that one person speaks and the other rebuts. Back and forth goes the argument. When they are not busy rebutting, they are refuting or interrupting or giving non-verbal signs that display impatience. These are the kinds of behaviours people engage in when they are afraid that they might come to really understand, and therefore, be forced to agree.

The process of understanding is one of the closest things I can think of as a "cure-all."

When people make the effort to understand they tend to find themselves probing the other person for more information . . . not in a questioning, confrontational manner, "What's that supposed to mean?", but in a gentle reflective tone such as "I'm not sure I fully understand; could you say more about what you mean?" They attempt to clarify what the other person has said by repeating back what they thought was communicated. When people are seeking to understand, it is as if two sets of eyes are fixed on the one soul. Both parties in the relationship focus on what one of them is attempting to communicate. They take for granted that the words may themselves not fully communicate the meaning of the communicator. Hence they have to take time to arrive at the meaning behind the words. It has been my experience that the process of understanding is one of the closest things I can think of as a "cure-all" in relationships. When people feel understood, it is often easier to tolerate disagreement. Understanding itself builds a closeness that allows relationships to grow. The next time you have a conflict on your hands, remember that understanding does not imply agreement. Without understanding, the relationship will not grow.

41

VULNERABILITY GROWS FROM A SENSE OF SAFETY

Carl Whitaker, a pioneer in the field of marriage and family therapy, told a story about psychotherapy which might just as well be told of a good marriage. When Whitaker was college-age, he had a good friend who was on the boxing team. Carl asked his friend to teach him how to box. So the friend took Carl up to the gym and fitted him with gloves. The friend then said, "Carl, swing at me as much as you want . . . you won't hurt me. When you put your guard down, I'll tell you about it!" In this way Carl could practice boxing with the knowledge that no one was going to get hurt. Knowing that no one is going to get hurt is a key element in building a climate within relationships that permits vulnerability. If intimacy is going to grow, relationship partners must feel that they can reveal as much of themselves as they know. Social psychology has taught us that to a large degree, that who we are as individuals is determined by our relations with others. It is "in relationship" that we best come to know ourselves. For example, in a group of shy people, you might be very assertive and take on a leadership role. In a more outgoing group, you might experience yourself as a follower. In this way you experience yourself as a "social self." But would the "real you" stand up.

Safety is a key element in resolving conflicts.

In order to know our "real selves" we usually need an atmosphere of safety where we can take the risks to try things that we have not tried before and know that we will not get hurt. This means that we would feel free to talk about the needs we have which might expose our vulnerability. If relationship partners take the risk of exposing their needs and then feel that this is in someway used against them, it is less likely that they will ever open themselves up again. When relationships provide safety so that people can be vulnerable, there are usually clear rules about confidentiality. You can tell your wife something and you know that she will not tell even her best friend. You should be able to tell your husband about your innermost needs and know that these would never be brought up "against" you in the course of even the most heated debate. Safety is a key element in resolving conflicts. Each partner in the relationship needs to feel that he or she can say what needs to be said without it being over-personalized or thrown back in retaliation . . . indeed it's very much like boxing with a friend who lets you throw punches that you know will not hurt and who tells you when your guard is down, but who never hits back.

42

The Reason For Unreasonable Fights

W hat can be more humiliating than for two mature people to find themselves at the tail end of a marital conflict over something that really does not matter at all? Toothpaste, the way the dishwasher is loaded, deciding what to do on Friday night, any one of these things may be trivial in the grand scheme of life. For some marital partners, for a brief moment in time, they take on ultimate proportions. Consider the movie *The War of the Roses*. A couple, once in love (both bright and talented people) find themselves involved in a divorce that reaches bizarre and finally tragic ends. At one point the husband, a usually sane, competent lawyer, makes a pate and tells his ex-wife it is made from her most treasured pet. The sad thing about the movie is that it is not pure fantasy. I swear, I've seen this couple in my office for divorce mediation on more than one occasion! Why is it that reasonable people engage in unreasonable fights? This is a complex mystery to which we can only give a few clues. Unreasonable fighting is a signal that the conflict is touching on emotions that are primitive and close to one's core sense of self. Some marital therapists would give the following interpretation; the trivial issue at hand has resurrected ancient feelings of rejection and abandonment against which there is a tremendous protest.

Unreasonable fighting is a signal that the conflict is touching on emotions that are primitive and close to one's core sense of self.

Fighting couples are no longer fighting about toothpaste . . . they are fighting the injury they felt when they were hurt as small children. They are no longer adults in conflict; they are six months old, or maybe two or four or six and they are saying, "I don't feel loved when my needs aren't met!" A second clue may have to do with what people have learned about control. If they have learned that the world is safer when everything is going their way, then they will likely fight ferociously to ensure the protection of their comfort zone. This leads to a third clue - personality styles. Certain kinds of personalties require a great deal more control over their environment. Vigilant personalities always like to be on top. If not, the world feels scary. In contrast, obsessive compulsives and their more healthy expression, the conscientious personality style, love order. When things are out of place they too feel threatened. If either of these types is married to a dramatic or adventuresome personality that finds order confining and hates to be controlled, the storm warnings are up! The point to all this is that when reasonable people engage in unreasonable fights, something much deeper is at stake. Professional therapy may be required.

43

DUCKING CONFLICT DOESN'T WORK

T here are certain kinds of people whose personalities demonstrate a phobia about conflict. Others avoid conflict because of what they experienced in their family of origin when growing up. Some may have lived in such angry and hurtful environments that to survive, it was necessary to lie low to dodge the bullets. These people are often paralysed by conflict. Some run away when conflicts arise. Some placate and do anything possible to appease those who are not happy. Whichever method is chosen, it usually does not work. Ducking, or avoiding conflict, may work in the short run, but in the long run, it seldom pays off. Consider a couple that deals with problems in their relationship by avoiding the differences behind the conflict. Her husband does not like her friends. Rather than be in conflict, she avoids the issue and gives up her friends. Her husband does not like her involvement in the church - she gives up the church. Her husband does not like her working - she gives up her job. You can see that this is a prescription for a nervous breakdown or a mid-life crises. A woman like this will soon lose her own identity. She likely will not recognize her resentment at her partner and this unrecognized resentment will contribute to her depression. One day she may say to her partner, " I just don't love you any more." He, for his part, will be surprised.

Avoiding conflict is a certain way to let the relationship die.

Because she avoided conflict he will have thought that everything was fine. Eventually he will realize that her being "easy going" or "acquiescing" to his will was a slow form of betrayal. Taking time out to cool down an out of control argument is an effective strategy to restore rational problem solving. Time out is not avoiding. Avoiding conflict is a certain way to let the relationship die. Creative conflict restores the intensity that healthy relationships require. By using good communication and problem-solving skills, conflict helps us to know ourselves and our partners better. Couples who refuse to avoid conflict, who face their conflicts and work them through, usually find that greater intimacy is achieved. In intimate relationships, it is always important to state your needs clearly and to work towards solutions that help each partner.

THE ARGUMENT THAT NEVER ENDS

Much of what we believe about conflict we have learned in our family of origin. I grew up in a family of British descent. We were a family of fumers. When there was serious unresolved conflict, the house went silent. In this way, conflict came to be associated with distance and tension. Silence meant punishment. If I'm angry, I won't talk to you. The worse your offense, the longer the punishment . . . very logical. Eventually the silence melted away, but without the initial conflict being resolved. Our next door neighbours were French Canadian. There was no logic there. When these people were angry, the whole neighbourhood knew it. There would be loud words, doors slammed, car tires screeching. Sometimes the husband's car would be gone for a night then back the next day. Once their anger had dissipated, they were able to be back together again, feeling good, but again without the initial conflict being resolved. Imagine what it would be like had I married the next door neighbour's daughter. When conflict arose, she might raise her voice. I would become silent to punish her. She, being dismayed by this behaviour, would raise her voice to get my attention. Surprised at her very bad behaviour, I would withdraw even more and vow to punish her with a longer silence. And so the pattern would escalate. No longer would the issue be the initial conflict; the issue would be the way each person attempted to resolve the conflict.

Unresolved conflict can have a cancerous effect on a relationship.

The dysfunctionality of these methods of conflict resolution can be seen in the fact that the initial reasons for conflicts never got resolved. In the short run, couples with a considerable amount of affection and good will can overlook the unresolved spots. Eventually though, these can have a cancerous effect on a relationship. The message taken from them may be one of failure. It is not surprising that people who come from families where conflict never got resolved may be prone to depression and pessimism. The solution is to develop a model of conflict resolution that ensures that all conflicts find some good outcome. Couples with a commitment to resolving conflict have an experiential approach to problem solving. They will try a solution for a while; if it doesn't meet the needs of each partner, they brainstorm new solutions. They might go back again to talk through the symbolism of the conflict. It may be that what they thought was the conflict; has a deeper meaning. There is an ancient adage, "Don't let the sun go down on your anger!" Here we might say, "Don't let your conflicts go unresolved!"

ON OVERPROTECTION

Good intentions sometimes go awry. There are times when you may agree to things in order not to hurt someone's feelings. People who are recognized as being "nice" people have an especially difficult time asserting their own wants and needs in a relationship. They fear that if they really speak their minds, it may be hurtful to their partner. Rather than hurt the one they love, they keep silent. Not saying anything in order to protect someone's feelings may be appropriate in some limited social situations. There are some thoughts that verge on the dark side of our personality which are better left unsaid. It is not helpful, for instance, to tell your partner you do not like a mole on her cheek. There is likely nothing she can do about it; she is likely highly sensitized to it anyway, and if she could change it, she would. Besides, it probably isn't much of a problem to you anyway. In marriage, not saying what you want will usually lead to further problems. People who don't say what they want for fear of hurting their partner, frequently use a conflict resolution strategy known as capitulating. Capitulating means giving in to the wishes of the other person and discounting your own. For example, your partner wants to borrow money to buy a new car. Even though you may be very uncomfortable about it, you ignore your own feelings and go along with your partner's wish.

People who don't say what they want for fear of hurting their partner, frequently use a conflict resolution strategy known as capitulating.

There are times when capitulating may help the relationship, but only when each partner is willing to capitulate on occasion and when this represents a minor number of the conflicts you resolve. Resentment and despair are the common by-products of capitulating. No matter how nice you are, if you let your needs get pushed aside, eventually resentment will start to build. If you as a couple never resolve conflicts in a way that produces solutions that are good for both of you, you may come to despair about your ability to build anything creative together. If capitulating is not the answer, then what is? Nice people need to accept that very often they avoid being assertive about their own needs because they fear that if they state them, they will not be met. It becomes an issue of trust. Many "nice" people have come to believe that they are acceptable as long as they are doing the giving, but they do not really expect others to "give" back to them. From this perspective, conflict resolution strategies become a self-esteem issue. "Nice" people need to believe that their partner wants to meet their needs, and must practice stating their desires without second guessing what the response might be.

A MODEL THAT WORKS

Although it is one of the most sensible things that relationship partners can do, most people have never done it . . . they've never sat down and consciously chosen a model for resolving conflicts. Thus it is unlikely that many couples have taken the time to actually practice the skills for resolving conflicts. Odd isn't it, that we put so little time into training for something that can have such a big impact on our lives. For the most part, we usually attempt to use the conflict resolution strategies we learned in our family of origin, whether or not they are adaptive to the current situation. What I would like to do here is to give you a framework for a rational model for resolving relationship conflict. You might want to consider whether or not your current way of solving problems has any of the following components. The first thing that is needed is time alone for reflection. It's important to think through your feelings. If you are angry, ask yourself, "What hurt is this anger based on?" Imagine how you might communicate your hurt without blaming your partner. If you're all steamed up, take a time out until you can communicate rationally. Once you understand something of your own position you need to set a time for discussion so that each partner feels equally ready. Make sure that this is not when your blood sugar is low (before eating for example), after you've been drinking or when you are tired and stressed out.

**Sometimes the model you find is the least expected,
and maybe, just a little far-out and crazy.**

When these steps are taken, it's time to determine the problem. This is when your communication skills are used. It's important to take time to figure out if there are any deeper levels to the issue at hand. Once you know what the problem is, brainstorm solutions. Do not prejudge any ideas. Think up crazy far-out solutions as a way of having fun and getting the juices flowing. Think of solutions that require only one person changing. Think of solutions that require both of you to change. From among your options, contract a solution. Make sure it is do-able, practical, behavioural and measurable. Take an experimental approach. "We'll try this for a few weeks; if it doesn't work, we'll try something else!" Finally, with this experimental mind set, establish a time when you will review your solution. If the conflict is not resolved, go back to an earlier stage in the process. This rational perspective has helped many couples come to a loving solution.

INVALIDATION: A PREDICTOR OF DIVORCE

H oward Markman, speaking at the 49th Annual Conference of the American Association for Marriage and Family Therapy, reported the results of a ten year, longitudinal study - three conflict resolution patterns predicted divorce. These patterns were withdrawal, escalation, and invalidation. The latter of these can be particularly destructive. Here's a case of invalidation. "Man, you are so stupid. How can you even think something like that?" Try a milder version, "You can't be serious! Your attitudes are really out to lunch!" Sure, these examples of invalidation are easy to spot, but very often in relationships, invalidation happens in more subtle forms. See if you can recognize the invalidation in this conversation. "John, I want to talk about our finances." "Hey, don't be so serious all the time! You always want to get into heavy stuff!" Did you see the invalidation? Try this one. "Joan, I want to have more quality time for us." Response - "Ever since you've got into that men's movement you're always pushing new ideas . . . why can't we be happy the way we used to be?" Do you recognize the invalidation here? Invalidation occurs as a common element of any relationship where we interrupt, block, frustrate or belittle the thoughts, feelings and wishes of another person. Expressions like, "you always," are the give away. These remarks invalidate by overdramatizing and making what may be a reasonable request, into something that sounds unreasonable.

A very subtle form of invalidation occurs when we don't take the time to listen to our partner's concerns when we have a conflict.

At times, invalidation can be seen when one partner will not take the other seriously. I have worked with couples when one partner used humour as a means to avoid serious conflict resolution. On other occasions it may simply be saying something like, "Hey, lighten up. Why do you have to be so serious, ALL THE TIME?" Did you notice the put down at the end? The whole statement is a put off - a socially acceptable refusal to engage the other partner, thus invalidating that partner's point of view. If this goes on too long, the partner that wants to work through a conflict will become increasingly hurt and dissatisfied. A very subtle form of invalidation occurs when we do not take the time to listen to our partner's concerns when we have a conflict. This can go from the extreme of doing something else, such as watching television or reading the paper when your partner is attempting to talk to you, to listening with a closed mind. Either way, your partner will get the message. What he or she thinks and feels is not important to you. Good relationships cannot afford invalidation. Pay attention to what you say and more importantly, pay attention.

Sexuality

MARRIAGE NEEDS ROMANCE AND SEX

opular thinking sometimes suggests that marriage requires work and commitment. That makes a lot of sense. There are so many obstacles from within the couple and without, conspiring to nullify a relationship, it seems appropriate that marriages need work. When the most prestigious family sociology journals predict that of those being married now, 50% will eventually divorce and a large number will be dissatisfied, it is clear that marriage needs work. The work of marriage should be directed toward effective communication, fairness in duties and responsibilities within the home, and appropriate conflict resolution. But marriage is more than just getting along like roommates. The soul of the marriage can be seen reflected in the sexual and romantic life of the couple. The romance and sex of marriage also requires work. What exactly is the "romantic" part of marriage? Although it is hard to pin down, romance has to do with the playfulness, the openness, the lack of control, the making of many "firsts," the eye contact, the wanting to be close in a non-confining way. Think of romantic scenes in movies. There is spontaneity and sometimes impulsiveness. There is walking on the beach in the rain, sending flowers unexpectedly, telling the world that you care about that person. Couples in love talk in flattering ways about each other, even in front of each other. A friend of mine who is very much in love with her boyfriend calls him her "sweetheart." She always smiles when she says it.

In love couples have secrets. They are deeply interested in what the other says. They remember small things that matter.

Unfortunately, couples often seek to avoid intimacy by developing a routine and predictable sex life. They make love at the same time, in the same way, for years. This is a reality that characterizes many marriages. This regularity may be comfortable, but it may deaden this potentially exciting, bonding dimension of marriage. I have found that it is not that unusual that couples coming for therapy have often stopped having sex altogether. Contrast this with couples who are in love. They talk about their fantasies, their likes and dislikes. They try making love new ways, they look forward to love making and concentrate time and energy on sex. Although some think that familiarity destroys sexual excitement, it need not. People change, and so do their needs. There is always room for new discoveries. The real blocks come from a lack of attention and the fear of closeness. So, work on your communication skills, make sure that the relationship is fair and resolve your conflicts as they occur. But above all, if you want the basis for a "love" marriage to remain intact, experience seems to show that you need to pay particular attention to those behaviours that keep romance and sex alive.

HAVING A REASON TO HAVE SEX

In the popular motion picture, *City Slickers*, actor Billy Crystal says to his friend something like "Men don't need to have a reason to have sex; women do." Although this blatantly sexist remark seems outdated and politically incorrect, it summarizes the experience of many marital partners. Sexual expression can be a particularly painful conflict. Perhaps it is the implicitly intimate nature of sex. Perhaps it is the cultural expectations we bring to it. Whatever it is, many couples have disappointments and anger related to sex. At the heart of these problems is the issue of affection. Women in counselling often report confusion when they believe that their partner can have a fight with them then go to bed and want to make love. For the woman the necessary conditions, the loving reasons for wanting to have sex, are not present. It seems it doesn't matter for her partner. This gives the woman a message that she isn't special. She doesn't feel that she is wanted because of their relationship, or that their sexual life is a part of a harmonious relationship. She feels dehumanized. On the other hand, many men feel manipulated and powerless about their sexual relationship. They fail to see that they have some control over their sexual relationship, in that they have the ability to affect the climate of the relationship. They can create the conditions that produce the "reason" for having sex.

The amount of sex in a relationship has to do with the amount of *affection* and *safety*.

The reasons for having sex vary, but seldom do healthy women want to have sex in a relationship where they don't feel safe. Men forget that safety means "emotional safety." This often isn't the same kind of concern to men, perhaps because male sexuality is not a "receptive" experience that implies as much vulnerability. Safety means you will not say hurtful things to me, that you can be respectful towards my feelings and consistent. Men who are "stable, solid types" are often confused when their wives say, "I can't trust you with my feelings." What they often mean is, "When I talk about my feelings, you don't seem to understand, you interrupt me, you give me advice, you don't really support me by listening." There are times when women need a sense of fun and romance in order to want to have sex. Often, however, the amount of sex in a relationship has to do with the amount of affection and safety. Many women in counselling report that they enjoy sex for the closeness as opposed to pure sexual pleasure. Many men share this experience. The point is clear: it is impossible to separate the development of love and affection from the issue of healthy sex in long-term relationships.

51

THE ADVENTURER AND THE TRADITIONALIST

Personality plays a major role in marital adjustment. This can be seen clearly concerning the issue of freedom to experiment sexually. Certain personality types gravitate towards adventure, experimentation and variety. Others are conservative, traditional and ritualistic. At times there is a gender difference when it comes to sexual freedom. Men have been socialized to feel freer about sex. Women have been cast in the role of preservers of conservative sexuality. These social scripts frequently invade marriages, with men believing their sexual life should be more adventuresome. A third important variable related to sexual experimentation is developmental stage. Researchers of human sexual response have long thought that male sexual interest peaks in the late teens and early adulthood, whereas female sexual interest is thought to peak as women enter their thirties. Consequently, a man with a high sexual interest at one stage of life, may have quite a different interest at another stage of life.

"Married" does not have to mean "boring."
"Monogamy" does not have to mean "monotony."

Life circumstances make a difference as well. It is not uncommon for young women in the early childrearing stage to report losing most of their interest in sex. In contrast, a man going through the "male menopause," may experience pressure to assert a sexual sense of self. All of these variables, personality, socialization, age and stage of life, mean that a couple in a long-term relationship will have to renegotiate their understanding of their sexual relationship several times. A major difference that goes unresolved, will cause considerable disruption to the couples intimacy. It is important for partners to reach a compromise. Those who want more experimentation need to respect the sensibilities of the less adventurous. Pressuring a partner into sexual activity with which they are not comfortable will do extensive damage to the quality of the relationship. On the other hand, it is important for both partners to realize that their sexual relationship can provide a format for variety that stimulates the playful intimacy of loving couples. Keeping this kind of romance alive will take some deliberate effort. To some people, this "planning for romance" seems paradoxical. Yet, there is a place for planned spontaneity and variety in sexual expression. The book *How to Make Love To the Same Person For the Rest of Your Life and Love Doing It*, suggests that the issue of sexual expression is one that can be resolved. "Married" does not have to mean "boring." "Monogamy" does not have to mean "monotony." Couples planning a long-term relationship need to openly consider the variables which affect this pivotal relationship dimension.

DIFFERING SEXUAL INTEREST

A husband brings his wife of thirty-five years a glass of water with two aspirin and says, "This is for your headache." She replies with surprise, "But I don't have a headache!" "I gotcha!", he retorts. This skit from the television show, America's Funniest People, illustrates a common problem in long-term relationships - differing sexual interest. It points to a second problem in long-term relationships - the need to talk honestly about sexual needs and desires. Needs and desires . . . it is important to remember that having sex is not a "need" on the same level as eating, breathing, and sleeping. It does, however, have a strong biological base, and therefore some people get confused and think that it is a need. I have met men in my counselling practice who have had the erroneous belief that they need to have sex every day. Usually this indicates a sexual problem which borders on obsession or addiction. Some say they can't sleep without sex. If this is true, it indicates a psychological, not a sexual, problem. A common scenario confronting many therapists is the adult survivor of sexual abuse who loses sexual interest. Since many women victims have denied and repressed their abuse, they present it as marital sexual problems, when in fact, they have their roots in past traumas.

A lack of sexual interest can be indicative of emotional and physical problems, as well as relationship problems.

Those who have seen the movie or read the book, *The Prince Of Tides,* will recall that the main character, played by Nick Nolte, had lost all interest in sexual contact with his wife. He had given up on a lot of things in life until he began to unravel the pain of his childhood. Couples who have the ability to communicate can quickly assess whether or not they are dealing with hyper or depressed sexuality. In either of these cases, they may want professional help. In many other circumstances, the differences will be less dramatic and not have a deep-rooted origin. In these cases it is important to bring a solution orientation to bear on the problem. Each partner should ask the other about their desires. In long-term relationships, sexual interest is often depressed by a lack of time together, conflict and incivility, over-familiarity, poor physical conditioning and worries about pregnancy. Each of these issues has to be addressed. Should the excitement and tenderness of sexuality safely be reserved for the uncommitted casual relationships we observe in the movies? It need not be. Although sexual relationships in marriage will evolve through various stages, each phase can offer pleasure and marital enhancement. The keys to maintaining a healthy sexual relationship are sensitivity, communication and a desire to find solutions that work for both parties.

TECHNIQUE OR TENDERNESS

T he movie *Basic Instinct* received a great deal of media attention for the uncensored portrayal of a psychopathic female murderer. Michael Douglas, who plays a tough dedicated cop, finds himself in a sexual relationship with the suspect. In so many words, he describes their sexual relationship as the sex of the century. You may also recall that this movie drew bands of protesters when it was first released, objecting to the way homosexuals were presented in this film. No one seemed to disagree with the assumption that the "sex of the century" was possible between two people who didn't like each other and were involved in a dangerous and callous pursuit. The media message about sexuality, from television ads to box office movies, seems to be that casual relationships are the context for having exciting sexual encounters. Marital sexuality continues to be the butt of tired jokes, suggesting that sex in marriage is dull and flat, if not a source for conflict. It is as if our basic instinct towards coupling is incompatible with other basic instincts. The pervasiveness of the Hollywood message can infiltrate even the most rational of minds. It's important then for married partners to face this challenge, lest they feel that they have surrendered their sexuality when they chose to stay married. The sexuality of the movies is based on the adrenaline rush associated with risk. In this case, it isn't sex that is exciting, it's risk. For some, this intoxicating feeling can become addictive.

Each partner has to examine his or her own sexuality first and then learn to share this information with their partner. Why leave open dialogue to Hollywood couples on the big screen?

Deprecating Hollywood sex does not automatically enrich marital sex. The first step is for couples to make a decision to prove the "dull marital sex" expectation to be wrong. Next, each partner has to examine his or her own sexuality. What are the conditions that make for sexual fulfilment? For some it will be safety, for others, variety. Where is it that you like to be touched? How do you feel about nudity? Is there a particular time of day when you are most interested in sex? These are questions that married partners often avoid. In counselling, couples tell me that they get into a rut. They have sex only in their own bed, in stereotypical ways, at regular intervals, usually when they are too tired. They think they know what the other thinks about sex, but seldom talk about it openly. Maybe this is where the movies can help us. Often in the movies, sexual partners seem to have an open dialogue. Like riders in a New York cab, their life is an open book. Given this kind of dialogue plus the tenderness and safety of a loving relationship, any couple should be able to enjoy "the sex of the century."

TALKING ABOUT SEX

T alking openly about sex on an ongoing basis is one way to ensure that this important relationship dimension remains a support to the loving intimacy of the marriage. It isn't always easy for partners to do this. A lack of ease in talking about sex likely indicates that the topic deserves considerable attention. It may be that one partner has a problem about sexuality which ought to be explored. Research on families has shown us that families that talk to their young about sex are unusual. At times mothers talk to their daughters about sex. Rarely does anyone, mothers or fathers, talk to their sons. This general societal taboo regarding open talk about sex in families suggests a pattern that many people carry into marriage. Who taught you about sex? If it was your parents, which it likely wasn't, were they at ease about it, or was there embarrassment and anxiety? What does it infer when families don't talk about sex, or do so awkwardly? Likely it suggests that sex is a taboo family topic. This same taboo often carries over to ensuing marital relationships. Add to this family awkwardness the mistaken belief that religion equates sex with sin, the large number of sexual abuses and improprieties, and the amount of emotional associations attached to sexuality, it is small wonder that many people have difficulty talking about their sexuality. This means that most marital partners who are serious about shaping their sex life need to expect that it will likely take time to be as comfortable talking about sex as they would other aspects of their relationship. It would be important to begin any sexual conversation by acknowledging this difficulty. Couples can then discuss a series of questions such as are found in any sexuality inventory which a marital and family therapist in your area should be able to supply. These questions could include:

1. **At this point in time, what helps you to feel sexual and to want to be close in a sexual way?**
2. **What seems to block your sexual desire?**
3. **What kind of beliefs have you acquired about sex that you would like to change?**
4. **Are there any sexual activities that are clearly a turn off?**
5. **In what ways do you think that you could be a more fulfilling partner to your mate?**
6. **In what ways could your mate be more fulfilling to you?**

As you talk about these questions, consider how you feel. What do your feelings tell you about your sexual attitudes? Is it highly charged? Are you defensive? Becoming comfortable talking about sex can ensure that it becomes an integral part of a loving marriage, not an awkward or habitual duty.

BEATING BANALITY

Although there are many well documented problems in marital relations today such as spousal abuse, alcohol and substance abuse problems, perhaps the largest threat to marital quality is banality. Banal relationships are those that have gone flat, like a soft drink left to stand with the lid off, some essential ingredient is missing. Banal relationships may continue to have the outward form of a successful marriage. The couple may still go to parties, have friends and family to visit, attend church, be good parents and yet be lacking any kind of heart-to-heart personal communication. As well there may be no tension caused by differences needing to be resolved or excitement resulting from new adventures being considered. I have known people who have been content with banal relationship for a long time, before they become aware of the vacuum that stands behind the banality. In counselling, people in banal relationships are often heard to say, "I love my partner, but something is missing." They feel guilty because they think about leaving the relationship and they aren't aware that they may have a legitimate reason for feeling this way. Certainly, if their mate was abusive, or alcoholic, they could understand, but in the case of banality, there seems to be no justifying rationale for feeling the way they do. In some cases this leads to self-blame, guilt and depression.

If they would allow themselves to experiment, simply for the sake of experimenting, some new adventures might emerge.

They may even go to a mental health professional seeking help for what they think are "individual" problems, but which are, in effect, marital problems. A well-meaning mental health professional may reinforce this "individual" perspective if they are not accustomed to analyzing personal problems from the family systems perspective. Banal relationships are depressing, but they can be changed. The first step would be to assess whether or not there are personal secrets, particularly about innermost thoughts and feelings which are not being shared, problems that are not being confronted. This is usually a major factor contributing to banality. A second major contribution to banality is a lack of new recreational/leisure stimulation. Think for a moment of what contributes to growth of love for new couples. Everything they do together is a first. Often they make efforts to go on interesting dates. They will try new activities for the sake of their new partner. Their life together is filled with new discoveries. If you were to interview most married couples, you would find that they seldom do anything new. If they would allow themselves to experiment, simply for the sake of experimenting, some new adventures might emerge. Banality is a preventable relationship affliction. Honesty, imagination, and a little effort can put the fizz back into a flat relationship.

Spirituality

RESPECT YOUR PARTNER'S BELIEFS

I n a book about family health, *No Single Thread,* psychiatrist Robert Beavers comments on a study of family health. Whereas much of the research about families focuses on dysfunctional families, Beavers chose a sample of families that were non-clinical and perceived to be doing well. In essence, he found that there was no single factor which differentiated healthy from dysfunctional families. The difference was a variety of qualities woven together into family strengths. One of these qualities has to do with spirituality. Beavers found that healthy families have a "respect for the experience of others." This fundamental respect for the autonomy of your partner can be demonstrated in the way religion and spirituality are handled within a marriage. Partners lacking respect for the autonomy of their spouse may mock or tease their spouse about their religious views. A more subtle form of invalidation is to attempt to ignore the religious convictions of a spouse, or even to sabotage their involvement with their faith community. The more "right" you need to be, the less space there is for your partner to have his or her views.

Taking your partner's spiritual and religious beliefs seriously is a significant gift of love.

Seldom, even within the same religious denomination, do any two people see everything the same way. This is not to say that truth is relative, but to say that people experience relative truth in their attempts to experience something absolute and transcendent. Your partner's beliefs about life will likely change over the course of your marriage. They may stay within the same religious faith, but their ideas may deepen and mature. You don't have to share your partner's ideas and beliefs to be a good partner. It is more important that you have great interest and respect for what they believe and take an ongoing interest in them. In many marriages, couples belong to churches without ever really talking about what they believe or how their views are changing. In some relationships, partners coexist. She goes to church, he doesn't. They never talk about it. In these cases, religion creates solitude. Couples often talk about the "big issues" of life when they are courting but never again. When they do this, they miss the chance to demonstrate respect for some of the most fundamental aspects of their mate. Remember understanding does not imply agreement. Taking your partner's spiritual and religious beliefs seriously is a significant gift of love.

A SHARED WORLD VIEW

ocial science often avoids religion. There is a fear that it is too subjective. Going where angels fear to tread, psychiatrist Robert Beavers, *Successful Marriage,* reports that "healthy marital partners have meaning that transcends their own skin and the boundaries of their family members. It may be provided by conventional religion or by a passionate cause . . . The content seems unimportant (at least to an observer), but having a belief that directs energy and provides community with others outside the family is vital." Beavers claims that this meaning system enables couples to deal with the inevitable losses of life, to respond to change with grace, and to have a sense of purpose. This sense of a bigger purpose in life is thought to be important to mental health and consequently has effects on the marriage. Couples who share similar belief systems are brought closer together by their view of the world. This doesn't mean that you have to have identical religious beliefs. A shared world view can be as basic as whether or not you both believe in conservation, or in balancing personal gain with community service.

Couples who share similar belief systems are brought closer together by their view of the world. This doesn't mean that you have to have identical religious beliefs.

Consider Philip and Janet. Philip is an entrepreneur. He has several businesses and likes to buy and sell real estate. When he has free time, he wants to spend it on holidays and recreational pursuits. Janet works as a secretary. She is involved with her church and several voluntary activities in the community. Philip resents it when he wants to do something with Janet and she has a voluntary commitment that conflicts. In these occasions he gets frustrated because he thinks she is wasting her time. He can't see how what she does helps the family. Janet has lost a lot of respect for Philip because she says he doesn't seem to have a social conscience. When it gets down to it, she thinks Philip only wants to live for himself; she thinks that people need to live for others and for what they can contribute. Surprisingly, they attend the same church. Janet and Philip are an example of a couple who have divergent world views. Their views are so different, they seem irreconcilable. It could be that they could try to understand each other and find common ground. If they don't, their marriage will really be a shell, not genuine. Likely there is so much hurt that neither really trusts the other any more. Janet will be vulnerable for fantasies of or affairs with men who share her social conscience and Philip may find himself attracted to other women who share his more openly hedonistic lifestyle. Starting married life with a common world view helps. Compromise and listening can help build consensus. Never should a couple underestimate the power of a shared perspective.

THE SLEEPER

North American society is largely tolerant of differing religious beliefs and expressions. This could led to the erroneous attitude that these things don't have much impact on intimate relationships. Shouldn't people of very different beliefs and values be able to fall in love, marry and be happy together? Theoretically, yes. In practice, differing values, beliefs and religious practices can be a sleeper. This means that couples in the early stages of love don't tend to take these differences seriously. Different spiritual orientations can lead to feelings of loneliness as well as the inevitable conflicts when partners are heading in mutually exclusive directions in life. Consider the simplest difference, a difference in religious practice. Tanis was raised in a "church attending" family. She believed in God but held moderate views, shared by her husband Ron. His experience of church was different though. His family had never attended a church and his father had thought that "church going" folk were too aggressive about their beliefs. He also thought that they were hypercritical. Although Ron had never had to think about it too deeply, this left him feeling slightly suspicious about "church people." In the earliest stages of their relationship, Tanis did not attend church. After the birth of their first child she wanted to attend church as a family. This became even more important after Tanis' mother died at the early age of 56.

One can see how family background impacts on spirituality.
Often these come into prominence only as people age.

Tanis felt disappointed and that her expectations were betrayed, even though Ron had never given any indication he would attend church. Church was a social as well as religious institution and she couldn't understand why Ron wouldn't support her, especially since she believed this would set a good precedent for their children. All she wanted was that he attend church. Ron felt that his autonomy was being challenged. Sundays came to be filled with overtones of disappointment, which Ron resented. He blamed the church. In Ron and Tanis's situation, one can see how family background impacts on spirituality. Often these come into prominence only as people age. Marriage partners in a rebellious stage of development from their families of origin might be dramatically drawn back to the faith of their fathers and mothers. Spirituality can become a strong uniting or alienating force within a relationship. It is difficult to predict what perspectives partners might take as the years go on. A general rule is that we gravitate towards the values of our families, unless we search out our own spirituality and cultivate practices that reinforce it. Sharing these practices can give a common viewpoint that unites, rather than separates the couple.

MAKING MEANINGS TOGETHER

T here is a certain perspective in the mental health field which is known as "social constructionism." In a nutshell, this perspective holds that the way the world appears to us is something that we ourselves have constructed. The world is not necessarily good, bad, filled with meaninglessness or inherently purposeful. Constructionists believe that the way we see it is the way we have constructed it. We don't do this alone, of course. Our families, our schools, our churches, our cultures help us to "construct" a social reality and fill it with meaning. There is a cartoon in which a man is kneeling down to propose to his girlfriend, and he says, " marry me Esther, and share my preconceptions." Social constructionists would like this cartoon and believe it describes what happens in marriage, political parties and religions. We come to see only from a certain view. One could get cynical, thinking about this constructionist view. Do we mean there is no "absolute reality," and that everything is relative and only has the meaning we subscribe to it? Constructionists might say yes, but they wouldn't say that each set of meanings has equal value.

If you want a firm foundation under you, keeping your spirituality shared and alive will help your marriage go the distance.

You can take a set of ideas, like you would a train. If you want to go to Chicago and you live in the west, you have to catch a train going east. It has been proven repeatedly, catching a west bound train from California won't get you very far. Certain ideas can be just as limiting and predictable in their outcome. In his book, *Man's Search For Meaning*, Victor Frankel, a psychotherapist who survived the war in a Nazi concentration camp for Jews, reports the "meanings" people made resulted in death or survival. His book is a testimony to the power of ideas and the therapeutic and survival value of making meaning in life. Couples in intimate relationships need to ask themselves, "Where are our ideas about life taking us?" Do we have values and beliefs that will see us through hard times, the loss of a job, the death of a loved one, problems raising children? Have we made meanings that allow us to be happy, whether or not we win the lotto, get a promotion, or get lucky in the real estate market?" This is what core spirituality adds up to in re- lationships. In some unfortunate couples, one makes optimistic meanings, while the other makes negative meanings. Usually this is not evident at first, but as time goes on, this basic spiritual difference shows and renders intimacy hard to find. In the busyness of relationships, it's easy to forget these fundamental questions. If you want a firm foundation under you, keeping your spirituality shared and alive will help your marriage go the distance.

MARITAL & SPIRITUAL HEALTH

L iving in a television world, we have come to realize that there are many differing religious beliefs on our planet. Is there any connection between these beliefs and marital health? Before you answer that question, consider another. Is there a connection between good mental health and healthy marriage? Then consider the connecting question, is there a relationship between good mental health and good spirituality? The answer to the last question seems to be that what is best in the great religions of the world tends to lead towards attitudes of care for oneself, others and the environment. Think of the commandments of Jesus, which boil down to "love God, love others, love yourself." You can't truly love yourself without having high self-esteem. This doesn't mean self-love or narcissism. Real self-esteem is not conceited. It is more like a quiet confidence and respect for oneself. That's what you would expect in someone who takes the "love others" part of the commandment seriously too. Cultivating a respect for the needs of others, as well as validating your own, leads to good social relations. It's obviously a good formula for an intimate relationship as well. A fully functioning person, from a mental health perspective, turns out to be very much like a fully functioning person from a religious perspective. Fairness, validating fundamental needs, respecting others, would be on the list for both.

> **The bottom line is that healthy religion and healthy**
> **mental health, both of which can contribute to a**
> **healthy marriage, need practice and support.**

Usually beliefs and attitudes need reinforcement. Human beings tend to absorb beliefs and attitudes almost by osmosis. Without some countering experiences, the prevailing culture of materialism can corrupt the most pious. The bottom line is that healthy religion and healthy mental health, both of which can contribute to a healthy marriage, need practice and support. This is a strong argument for every couple finding a spiritual home, a religious association that continually reinforces beliefs that you think are important to the way you want to conduct yourself and your relationships. Premarital couples often undervalue the importance of a religious association. They fail to see that to not find some group to associate with, will leave their attitudes and beliefs vulnerable to the ethos of contemporary culture. If contemporary culture does not support healthy relationship values, it may play a detrimental role. Every person in a serious relationship should ask themselves: "in what way am I reinforcing sound relationship and mental health practices?" Likely there is a religious community that could help you. Finding a comfortable fit for both of you, early in the relationship, will be an investment with long term dividends.

Family
Backgrounds

EMOTIONAL TEMPERATURE

T here are times when we don't know ourselves very well. For example, Joan and Jim have a conflict about the amount of affection in their relationship. Jim has developed a theory about this. He believes that Joan is a cold person. He believes that she intentionally avoids closeness. As for himself, he assumes that his desire for affection is "normal." What Jim doesn't know, is that what he thinks is "normal," is what he experienced in his family of origin. What he experiences from Joan, is the emotional climate in her family of origin. Her behaviour is no more intentional than his. She's just doing what comes naturally. Jim and Joan come from families with different emotional climates. In Jim's family, his mother was a warm effusive woman. She still hugs him when ever she sees him, and she hugs him whenever they part. In Joan's family, people seldom touch. Displays of emotion are infrequent and awkward. Joan would say that people in her family love each other; they just don't think that they have to make a big show of it. If Jim and Joan were to reflect on it, they might discover that the attraction they felt towards each other was based on a desire to modify the emotional temperature in their world. Although he now complains about Joan's coolness, when he first met her, this same quality appeared to be strength and independence, qualities that he didn't see in his mother. At times he felt that his mother's affection was overbearing.

In reality, each person is seeking to find the emotional climate they were used to in their growing up.

For her part, Joan was attracted to the emotion she saw being expressed in Jim's family. In small, dating doses, it filled some needs not met by her family. Once she began to live with Jim, she found his expression of emotion to be a demand for emotion. Jim's closeness seemed to invade her personal boundaries. The more he wanted closeness, the most claustrophobic she felt. Jim and Joan have reached that destructive point in their relationship, where they have begun to think that their partner's preferences are meant to hurt them. In reality, each person is seeking to find the emotional climate they were used to in their growing up. They are attracted to the familiar. The familiar often feels comfortable. The negative mind set Jim and Joan have assumed will damage their marriage. If they understood that our emotional comfort zone is related to our family backgrounds, they could get free of the blaming and start building. Jim and Joan could likely find a compromise that allows them to establish an emotional climate that both find acceptable.

Negotiating Togetherness

How important was "togetherness" in your family of origin? In some families, there is a high premium on togetherness, all the time. Children aren't expected to grow up and go away. They may marry, but they are to stay close. You may recall the movie, *The Godfather*. This is a family that prizes loyalty and togetherness over other values. In some families, togetherness means wearing matching knit sweaters, going on great holidays together, watching television every night. In other families, togetherness may mean a party every time there is a wedding or a funeral. Families differ in the amount of interaction between family members. Some families expect loyalty to their spirit of togetherness even after their young marry. In these cases, the family doesn't let go. It subsumes the new in-law into their network. In other families, large amounts of distance are tolerated. Parents have their own recreation. Friendships are kept separate from the family. Many of the problems couples have are related to loyalty to one's family of origin. If you have ever felt that your partner's family is more important to them than your marriage, then you understand the problem.

If your family styles are radically different in relation to "togetherness" and "loyalty," this is an issue you had better take lots of time to discuss.

How can people start a new family and still remain a member of the one they came from? This issue often becomes clear around holidays, such as Christmas. Most newly weds have to come to some decision about where and how they will spend Christmas. Summer holidays is another important choice point. Marital partners who come from decidedly different experiences of family togetherness will often have conflicts about the amount of time they spend with their in-laws, or the amount of time that they spend together. It is important to know that people from "togetherness" families are likely to continue to value togetherness and to experience autonomy as disloyalty. People who grew up in families with low togetherness and high independence, will feel hemmed in by too much togetherness. Togetherness and issues of loyalty to one's family of origin can lay dormant for many years in a marriage, only to be activated by death, accident or crises. Think of the case of the oldest son who moved to be closer to his mother after his father died. He never thought to consult his wife about it. It just had to be done. If your family styles are radically different in relation to "togetherness" and "loyalty," this is an issue you had better take lots of time to discuss.

YOU LEAD, I'LL FOLLOW

hen someone says, "you lead, I'll follow," who's in charge? Is it the one who leads, or the one who has told that person to lead? This type of saying points out the inter-dependent nature of relationships. The role one person plays in a marriage is dependent on the other person assuming a complimentary role. Every leader needs followers. If the followers refuse to follow, the leader is out of business. An abuser needs a victim. If an abused spouse gets help to get out of this position, through a woman's shelter, you can bet that this will throw the abuser into a crises. If a man assumes that he will control the finances of the family, this only works in as much as his wife allows him to do this. Whether they realize it or not, every married couple comes to an agreement on who will lead and who will follow. In some relationships, leadership may seem to come from the man. In other relationships, the wife may determine who they will socialize with, how they will spend their money, where they will live. Healthier couples find a way to share leadership, so that neither person feels subservient to the other. Decisions on who will lead and who will follow are often determined by family backgrounds.

**Decisions on who will lead and who will follow are
often determined by family backgrounds.**

What kind of a role would you expect a fairly passive woman from a father dominated household to play in marriage? Easy. She will comfortably fit into a husband lead household. What about an extroverted young man from the same household? That's easy too. He will expect that his wife will bow to his expectations. It gets more complicated, however. What role would you expect a woman from a father dominated household, would play, if she were involved in massive power struggles with her father? She might marry a man who has a high need for control, and then wrestle him for leadership. Or, conversely, a young man who grew up in a mother dominated household might marry a strongly directed young woman and then battle her for control. The point here is that our expectations about leadership in relationships are often set from observing how our parents resolved these issues. We tend to recreate scenarios from our past. As in the cases mentioned above, these re-enactments come with all the same emotions and dilemmas. Partners who marry someone whose family script is complimentary to their own, may seem to make a perfect fit. Unfortunately, often these "complimentary fits" limit the potential of each partner and consequently the relationship. Shared leadership offers the challenge for each partner to use their talents to provide direction for the marriage.

TWO SOLITUDES: CHAOS AND RIGIDITY

Sharon grew up in a home full of regimentation and structure. Her father, a sergeant major in the army, often brought his "Mr. Military" role into the home. Picture their house. Impeccable. The living room doesn't look lived in. Mr. Military made all the important decisions. Sharon's Mom had a limited sphere that included shopping, cooking, cleaning and minding the children. Discipline was Sharon's dad's job. Sharon's family would be described as a "rigid" family. Things don't change much. Life is predictable. There is a regularity and sameness that is stifling. In contrast to Sharon's home, Robert's could be described as chaotic. Things are never the same. His parents have a tempestuous relationship with many fights, breaking ups and getting together again. When his parents weren't functioning well, Robert's older sister, Karen, took responsibility for the home. There were times when his parents would seem competent and in control, and other times when they acted irresponsible. Alcohol played a major role in this instability. In Robert's home, leadership was often changing and at times children were given the responsibility and freedoms of adults. Robert's family is a picture of a chaotic family structure. Each of these family profiles are considered by family experts to be problematic. Rigid families usually stifle initiative and creativity. Extreme rigidity frequently provokes teenage rebellion. In chaotic families, there is so much freedom, that children lack the structure to be child-like, and thus appear to grow up fast, forfeiting the chance for sheltered maturing. Chaotic homes will often produce children who quit school and enter serious intimate relationships early.

A person from a chaotic family may yearn for structure and certainty, and fall in love with a person from a rigid family.

In the movie *Paris Trout*, the main female character marries a sadistic, paranoid wealthy small town business man. In reflection on why she married him she says, "there was a certainty about him that I was missing at that time in my life." This is an example of opposites attracting. A person from a chaotic family may yearn for structure and certainty, and fall in love with a person from a rigid family. Soon they will find this "rigidity" to be controlling, confining and claustrophobic. The person from the rigid family background may be attracted to what seems like the spontaneity and freedom of the person who is accustomed to a chaotic home-life. Eventually the person from the rigid background comes to think of their partner's former "spontaneity" as "irresponsibility," their "creativity" as "undependability." A general rule for marriage is the more dissimilar the family backgrounds, the more work that needs to be done. Think about how your family operated and how your spouse's family operated. A fruitful discussion can emerge as you analyze your families on the continuum of rigid to chaotic.

HAVE THE DECENCY TO CONSULT ME

Often it is not the decision that marital partners make that hurt or help the marriage, but how the decisions are made. One of the most damaging patterns for marriage is making decisions without consulting your partner. This is the husband who quits his job, buys a car, invites friends for supper, goes for a drink after work, without checking with his spouse. It is the wife who invites her family for dinner, takes a job, a tells her friends about a family problem, without consulting her husband. Usually, these types of inconsideration are thoughtless . . . they aren't intentional. Seldom do people say to themselves, "I think I'll miss supper with the family in order to make it difficult for my partner" or "I'm going to spill the beans about our problems to my friends, because I know that it will threaten my spouse." The cumulative effect of much thoughtlessness is to make the offended partner think that it is being done to them on purpose. One single large failure to consult can create the same effect. Think of Henry. He made a decision to quit his job without discussing this with his fiancee. She felt hurt that he hadn't consulted with her, but didn't say anything because she didn't think she had the right, as they weren't yet married. She continued to resent his not consulting, and, two years after they were married, hit the roof when she overheard Henry telling a friend that he was thinking of quitting his job again.

Consulting one's partner is an important relationship behaviour.

Henry was stunned by the force of her reaction. Henry had grown up in a father dominated family. He was used to his dad making the decisions, as did many fathers of his era. As well, his family had a disengaged pattern. Family members frequently made plans without consulting others. His wife came from an enmeshed family. There were no secrets, no private plans, no unilateral actions. In her family, acting without consulting represented disloyalty. Changing the dynamics of this problem wouldn't be easy. Even if Henry understands Donna's need for consultation, he is apt to inadvertently act without consulting. Donna may know that Henry does not intentionally attempt to hurt her by not consulting, yet this doesn't stop her hurt when it happens. Their situation does suggest several ways to analyze a marital problem: - assume your partner is not intending to hurt you, assume that they are acting from patterns they have learned from years of living with their family of origin, assume that fundamental changes in behaviour take time. Consulting one's partner is an important relationship behaviour. Because it isn't always automatic, it's important for partners to establish consultation as a goal to work towards.

Family & Friends

YOUR RELATIONSHIP AFFECTS OTHERS

P arents often forget that the love and respect they have for each other can have a profound impact on the lives of their children. Recently, while giving a marriage enrichment week-end, a man told me the following story. The story emerged after I had been mentioning that many couples, who have difficulty sharing their feelings face to face, do so by writing letters to each other. Many people find that on paper they can get past their persona, and write about their real feelings. This man's father had died, followed years later by his mother. While the family was going through their mother's personal belongings after her death, they found a cache of personal letters, which the man's father had written to their mother. The father had worked away from home frequently. Instead of phoning, he would write his wife. She saved the letters to her dying day. The sons and daughters, finding this cache of memories, took the opportunity to read through them. They found them full of tender words that expressed the deep feelings their father had for their mother. The man said, "This was a side of dad we had never known." I asked this man to share this story with other people on the enrichment week-end. When he did so, his voice filled with emotion, as if he might cry at any moment. Through these old letters he had come to know something about his dad.

Even those who are divorced need to realize that the cooperation, respect and regard they give there ex-mate, will have an impact on the lives of their children.

His tears were tears of joy, and a sense of fulfilment, knowing of the love that his father had for his mother. His story seemed to be moving to the whole group. I made the point, that it is very healing for children to know that their parents care for each other. Most healthy parents want the best for their children. Parents often forget that children usually want the best for their parents. They want to know that their father treats their mother with kindness and respect and visa versa. So much of a child's self-esteem rests on this relationship. Often, children of dysfunctional parents make efforts at what appears to be rescuing their parents. The theory is that they want to make sure their parent is okay, so that the parent can then look after their child needs. Even in situations of divorce, I have found that although children will often resist a step-parent out of loyalty to their non-present parent, they are usually appreciative of a new spouse if that new person seems to make mom or dad happy. Unfortunately, parents frequently fail to notice this unsolicited caring and see only the resistance. This story is a lesson to all married couples with children. Even those who are divorced need to realize that the cooperation, respect and regard they give their ex-mate will have an impact on the lives of their children.

70

KINSHIP INTIMACY

T here are many different kinds of intimacy. Emotional intimacy suggests that a couple has a deep understanding of the feelings of each other. Recreational intimacy is the kind of closeness people get from sharing a common pleasurable pursuit. I imagine it is what hockey players feel as they pile up on each other after winning an important game . . . a kind of, "together against adversity." Many couples have a love of the same pursuits and this shared interest brings them together. Work place intimacy is similar. This is the kind of implicit understanding that one doctor has for another, what two clergymen from the same denomination can share. They have a sense that no one else quite fully understands the pressures they are under; this deepens bonding. Kinship intimacy has to do with sharing a common sense of family. Often you will hear people say that they are better known by their friends than by their family. And yet, there is a special sense of closeness that people from families share. Often, long time marital partners have this kind of intimacy. They have been so long together, they become a part of the extended family of each other. This of course adds an extra element of tragedy to divorce, as not only two people, but whole families are divided in their loyalties and often the whole family experiences the loss of one of the spouses. Sometimes it is this "kinship" intimacy that will carry a couple through thin times in other aspects of their intimacy.

Kinship intimacy is just one part of building a loving relationship. Often it is the momentum that keeps many relationships together.

For example, at a recent marriage workshop I was giving, a woman told me that she and her husband had recently gone through some rough times. She recalled however, that when her father was elderly and dying, that her husband had looked after him with tender devotion. She recalled her husband literally carrying her father where he needed to be. She said, "I just remember that image of him, being so tender with my dad, and I can't be mad at him." This is an example of "kinship" intimacy. No one else, no matter what they had to offer, could ever have shared that intimacy from sharing this woman's feeling for her father in his last days. Kinship intimacy is just one part of building a loving relationship. Often it is the momentum that keeps many relationships together. It can be much richer, if, like the woman who remembered the image of her husband caring for her father in his dying days, relationship partners can focus on the nostalgia and closeness that comes through "belonging" in this extended family sense. Intimacy in relationships is strengthened in many ways. Acting loving towards your partner's loved ones, is one way to strengthen a relationship.

EXCLUSIVELY YOURS

Exclusivity. Don't tell me you don't know what it means. Remember that crush you had in grade school that turned into a heart ache when you found they "liked" someone else. Do you recall going away on holiday, to return to find your steady had been flirting with someone else? If you remember anything like this, you know what exclusivity is all about. Rationally it may not make sense. In those heady days of the 60's people talked about "open marriage." This meant married partners should feel free to have multiple relationships. It may have been rational, but it really didn't work. When it comes to love, exclusivity continues to have a strong appeal. Exclusivity is the desire to matter most to someone, to come first. Exclusivity is a part of the feeling of romantic love. It has to do with being highly valued, considered precious, being wanted. It means that you are chosen among competing values. You can be sexually faithful, without having exclusivity in a relationship. There is the man who seems to value his sports more than his marriage. He says he loves her, and yet she does not feel like a high priority. Work seems to take on passionate qualities for many people, leaving their partners feeling "second," and definitely not exclusive.

It's important in any intimate relationship to be sensitive to your partner's need to feel that you want them, exclusively.

A common place where men lose their sense of exclusivity has to do with their partner's female friends. Historically, women have formed stronger intimate relationships with friends. One non-verbal man admitted that he was reluctant to share secrets with his wife because he had no sense of how exclusive it would be. Could he count on her not to gossip about him? Many marital partners of many years reach a point where they have many things shared . . . children, a house, cars, friends . . . they have a life together. They may still respect each other, but do they really still want each other? Are they in the marriage because of their history, family and belongings, or are they wanted primarily for themselves? Would they still choose each other? It is common for couples around the empty nest stage to be asking these questions. Translated it means, do we still have our exclusivity in love? Wanting to be wanted for oneself in an intimate relationship is a normal human desire. It is at the basis of the momentum towards coupling. It's important in any intimate relationship to be sensitive to your partner's need to feel that you want them, exclusively. As one man recently said to me, "Why do I have to tell her I love her . . . talk is cheap?" He may have a point. However, I'm with Teveh from the musical *The Fiddler on the Roof,* who says to his wife, "After 25 years, it's nice to know."

CUTTING THE CORD

It has been said that our families give us roots, and they give us wings. The wings part has to do with the normal process of setting the young free to form new families of their own, completing the cycle of life. Some families have difficulty with the wings part of this "roots and wings" equation. It has been said that one way to build love in a marriage is to act lovingly towards your partner's family. Another way is to demonstrate that your partner comes first, before your family of origin. In actuality this will likely take time. Perhaps in the first bloom of romantic love, it seems natural that your lover would come before your family. As times go on, it is not unusual for our loyalties to our family of origin to emerge, stronger than ever. Consider Terry's situation. His wife has a large family that have been known in the community for their closeness. There are endless rounds of family celebrations and events. Every Sunday is reserved for family gatherings. Often, the family holidays together. Terry comes from a more detached family, and he often feels overwhelmed by the togetherness of his spouse's family. He wishes that they could have more private times, together as a couple, and together as a family, just with their own kids. He finds himself resenting her family, and yet feeling ashamed of himself for feeling this way. His efforts to bring this up are treated as a heresy. Could it be that his spouse has not really "cut the cord?"

The art of the matter is to strike a balance, where the new relationship gets first priority, while maintaining a meaningful connection with the old.

In the inevitable round of hurt feelings following this kind of scenario, his wife will likely feel distant from Terry. She will say things like, "He's over-reacting" or "He doesn't understand what my family mean to me . . . just because his family isn't close doesn't mean he should be jealous of my family." Terry will feel misunderstood. He will begin to compare his spouse's love for him with the love she has for her family. He will imagine that he is "second" to her family. Terry and his spouse will have to find some way to validate his desire to feel like she would choose him over her family. After all, her future is with him. They might move away for awhile together; they might slowly increase their own family time, creating just a bit more distance from her family. Terry will have to be sensitive to how difficult this might be for her. She will have to understand the importance of "cutting the cord." Some families exude what has been called a centripetal force, an invisible power pulling children back towards the middle (the parents). The art of the matter is to strike a balance, where the new relationship gets first priority, while maintaining a meaningful connection with the old.

73

FITTING FRIENDS

Sometimes it is hard to accept your partner's friends and family. This lack of acceptance could be based simply on jealousy. Partners who feel inadequate seldom want to share their loved one with anyone else. There are times, however, when this dislike goes beyond jealousy, and this is may be a serious indication of trouble in the relationship. Friendships express something of our values. To a degree, we are a reflection of our friends and of their interests. Consider the case of the man who loved racing cars, in which his partner had little interest. He would want to get together with friends who also loved cars. He felt bored and out of place visiting with her friends. Every Christmas and June they had fights over his lack of participation in her staff parties. He just didn't feel like he fit in. He said he liked her friends, but didn't really feel comfortable with them. Although early in the relationship she had made efforts to share his interest in cars and sports, her enthusiasm waned. At times he felt that she was interfering with his having a good time.

**Sharing friends and being valued by your partner's family
will strengthen the prognosis for a relationship.**

It is natural for people to enter relationships bringing old friends with them. It is a wise policy to treat these long term friends of your partner with great respect. Whatever you might see as the flaws in them, it will be important to look beyond these and focus your attention on the positive qualities that draws your partner to them. A friend who seems like a boor, might have outstanding qualities of loyalty through adversity. A lethal mistake would be to put your partner in a position where they think they need to choose between you and their friends. It would be wiser to "go with the flow" and attempt to slowly develop a core of mutual friends that you both can enjoy. The story of Romeo and Juliet portrays love that should be free to survive outside of the conflicts and loyalties of families and friends. Their tragic end is no surprise. Statistics on relationship would indicate that few marriages last when they are unsupported by family and friends. This might be a key consideration for people in the early stages of relationships, when it is relatively easy to end the relationship. If their taste in friends is so different, this may mean that there is a basic incompatibility which would cause problems. Conversely, sharing friends and being valued by your partner's family will strengthen the prognosis for a relationship. Good friends mediate, counsel and encourage their friends to think twice when they are being hard to get along with in a marriage. Shared friends can bring a couple together, almost as shared love for children can bring parents together. Consciously developing friendship with couples who share your values will add to the strength and enjoyment you have in your relationship.

THE ROMEO & JULIET EFFECT

Romeo, Romeo! Wherefore art thou Romeo? Deny thy father and refuse thy name; or, if thou wilt not, be but sworn my love, and I'll no longer be a Capulet." The words of Juliet from Shakespeare's *Romeo and Juliet* suggests that the possibility of romantic love exists without the independence of love from the approval of one's friends and families and still seems popular in our society. But what actually does happen to a relationship as a result of the opinions of outsiders? Romantic love has long been of interest to family social science, perhaps because romantic love is considered a prerequisite in mate selection in most industrialized cultures. If you aren't in love, why get married? Well, millions of people in arranged marriages throughout the ages could answer that, but it seems to hold that weddings in our culture are a celebration of romantic love blossoming to a life-time commitment. But can romantic love exist without the support of both family and friends? Does it matter at all what others think?

Less well known is that parental support and the favourable opinions of friends are a positive predictor of the relationship continuing.

The answer seems to be a definitive, yes! Where would you go to test these things, but to a university, of course! Studies of dating college couples have found that interference from parents can actually fuel romantic love. This is known as the Romeo & Juliet effect. Less well known, is that parental support and the favourable opinions of friends are a positive predictor of the relationship continuing. The disapproval or apathy of either family or peers towards the relationship becomes a predictor of an affair that is destined to go nowhere. Although there may be some relationships which flourish and continue despite lack of approval from others, for the most part, the future of romantic entanglements seem to be closely related to what the important people in our lives think of them. Anyone entering a new relationship needs to take seriously what their parents, peers, or even their children, in the case of blended families, think of the new romance. If they don't approve, they can be ready for a rough go of it.

MY SPOUSE . . . MY FRIEND

Weddings are a great opportunity to learn something about love and family relationships. While "back home" for the wedding of my younger sister, I decided to do some field research. My sister had chosen a bulletin cover, popular at weddings these days, which said simply "Today I will marry my friend." She chose a reading from Kahil Gibran's book *The Prophet,* a selection entitled "On Friendship" to be read along with the traditional Bible readings. It seemed fitting, since she and her fiancee had been dating for seven years; they seemed as much friends as lovers. Another of my missions for "going home" was getting closer to my older brother. Fourteen years ago he was involved in a very messy divorce from which he wound up married to the "other woman." This was a major trauma to my conservative family. I had wondered how this second marriage, now twelve years old, was going. You'd think that would be easy to ask, but it wasn't. It isn't polite to simply walk up and ask someone something like, "So, was it worth going through that divorce, did you get what you want, are you still in love with your new wife, are you satisfied or even excited about your marriage?" At least, this isn't considered polite to ask in my family.

"Your friend is your board and your fireside."

This reveals another dynamic about marriage. What you see on the *outside* sometimes gives hints of strengths or weaknesses on the *inside,* but outside appearances often belie the real story. Only the people in a marriage really know how it is going. I know this is true, even though as a marriage therapist I think I'm pretty good at identifying marital quality by external cues. With this caveat in mind, I wanted to get it straight from my brother's mouth. Unfortunately, the busyness of the wedding festivities left no time for me to be alone with my brother to ask these sensitive questions. In desperation, while at the wedding reception, sitting beside my brother's wife, I attempted to scratch the surface with her. When I asked her what her life was like in the city in which she lives, she went through the usual sociable talk about her job, her interests, and then she said, "and I like to spend time with my friend," pointing to my brother across the table. She said, "We spend a lot of time together and like it." When she said it, I don't think she was conscious of choosing the word "friend" because of having heard it at the wedding that day, but simply because it fit her experience. It felt like I had my answer about their marriage. After all the anguish of his divorce, he and his second wife had come through it as friends. It reminded me of Gibran's words, "Your friend is your board and your fireside," someone who is a strength and support. My brother didn't have this in his first marriage. I felt a sense of comfort that he now did, and wished that every married person could say the same.

THE OPTIMISTIC COUPLE

T he way we explain events has a lot to do with how we feel about them, and the consequences that emerge from them. Athletes have taken this seriously for a long time. Many have psychologists who help with their mental conditioning. So why not use the same mental conditioning for couples in intimate relationships? In his popular book, *Learned Optimism,* Martin Seligman outlines the skills necessary for avoiding pessimism and pessimism's travelling companion, depression. If couples could learn these skills and share a common optimistic explanatory style, one would think that they would be better equipped to overcome many of the adversities which assail couples in long term relationships. Seligman claims that we get into problems when we explain an adversity as being pervasive, permanent, and personal. In contrast, when relationship partners are able to see difficulties as being temporary, specific and external to their worth as persons, they cope better and usually overcome adversities. Consider the example of Henry and Judy. Henry seems preoccupied with his work. They no longer have the long talks and great dates they once had. As with most couples, this pattern developed slowly and so went unnoticed until it had become a problem. If Judy was to take a pessimistic outlook she would say to herself, "He doesn't care about me anymore" (pervasiveness); "I'll never find a man who is really there for me" (permanence); "I'm a loser" (personalization). You can imagine the consequences of this kind of thinking. Judy is bound to act defeated, discouraged and as if she has given up on the relationship. This will likely impact Henry and he will be less inclined to want to spend time with her.

If Judy were to approach this from an optimistic perspective, she would acknowledge the problem, but she would not personalize Henry's behaviour.

Instead of thinking less of herself, she might think that Henry's preoccupation with work has something to do with issues in his life. Maybe he is feeling under a lot of pressure to be "the good provider." His negligence of the relationship may be because he is trying to "look after" the relationship in other ways. The optimistic view would have Judy acknowledging that although she doesn't like what is happening, it can be changed; it doesn't have to be permanent. This will help her to approach Henry with a more open mind, which will reduce his defensiveness. Instead of seeing his inattention as pervasive, it may be that he is not as attentive as he used to be, but there may still be ways that he is attentive to her that she hasn't been noticing. The pervasiveness of the pessimistic outlook may have blinded her to the things that Henry was doing right. She'll get further with Henry if she can let him know that she sees some positive things in his behaviour. This will make Henry more willing to work on the problem, which will likely set a positive tone for their relationship to change.

77

HONOURING YOURSELF

A key element of healthy relationships seems to be that each partner has a sense of his or her own worth. People without a strong sense of self-worth often feel and act dependent or controlling. Jesus taught that people should "Love thy neighbour as you love yourself." This saying is sometimes thought of as a call to self-sacrifice and self-denial. Another interpretation is that unless you really love yourself, not in a conceited, self-absorbed way, but in a way that is self-nurturing, then you won't have much to give to others. You can't love unless you have first been loved and have love for yourself. There are certain times in an intimate relationship when a person is apt to feel less self-affirming. Some of these times are related to predictable life stages, others can be tied to unpredictable life events. It is in these times that a person has to have a little extra help from their relationship partner, or that they should reach out to others for help. For example, women in the early child rearing stage commonly have a sense of lowered self-esteem. They willing sacrifice many of the elements of their life that gave them a sense of freedom and identity. In contrast the men in their life seldom make the same sacrifices. A common scenario is the man working all the harder to support the family, with his hard work bringing him external rewards and recognition. He seems to maintain his freedom and his "self." One young mother said to me, "I became known as my child's mother, not myself." Without the proper encouragement to get out and maintain a sense of self apart from the child, the young mother can slip into a low level depression and resentment of her spouse.

**If you honour yourself, it means you will have
all the more to give to others."**

The mid-life years of the early 40's are often difficult for men as they take stock of their life in a new way. A similar kind of life evaluation occurs for women reaching their 30's. These times of self-questioning can become times of self-doubt and lowered self-esteem. This in turn will have an impact on their ability to be loving and giving towards their partner. If we are to take responsibility for our own self-worth then what are we to do? It seems that there are many strategies with a few clear guidelines. The first is not to blame anyone else for the way we feel. Your spouse may contribute to how you feel, but they don't control it. If it belongs to you, *you* can change it. Another guideline is that you need to motivate yourself to do things that make you feel like you are learning, developing and expanding. You will need to do things that separate you from the significant people in your life (for example, your children or your spouse) that identify you as being autonomous. Finally, when you look after yourself, it is important not to "guilt" yourself for doing so. If you honour yourself, it means you will have all the more to give to others.

MEASURING A MARRIAGE

W hat is a successful marriage? Researchers of the family have struggled with this question for many a decade. The question has become more complex with time. Three contenders vie for prominence in the measurement of marital success - marital stability, marital quality and marital satisfaction. Marital stability refers to the predictability of the marriage, its lack of fluctuation, and that the couple can be counted on to be together. The marriage would be unshakable. It may not be a great marriage, there may not be a lot of romance and affection, but, like the farmer in the Norman Rockwell painting, standing with his pitch fork beside his wife, there is a sense that it is rock solid. The downside of high stability is complacency. Stability can lead to taking someone for granted, leaving a shell of a real marriage. A "stable marriage" that has a poor marital quality, can be soul destroying for the couple and their offspring. Marital quality refers to variety and stimulation within the marriage. Is there a rich dialogue between the companions? Do they communicate well? Do they do interesting things? Do they have common interests? Is there a sense of personal growth flowing from the marriage? Marital quality can, like stability, be measured from the outside. It is especially shocking when people learn that their friends who seem to have high marital quality, split up.

Whether they know it of not, couples make a decision about which criteria they will use to judge their marriage.

This only demonstrates that it is possible to be in an enriching environment and still be missing some other important ingredient to ensure a successful marriage. Marital satisfaction is the most subjective of all the criteria of success. Only the individuals within the marriage can judge this. What is satisfying to one may not be to the other. A person can be in a seemingly stable, rewarding marriage, and yet not feel deeply satisfied. The marriage may be lacking the depth of intimacy that one finds in a "soul mate." Feeling satisfied with the marriage has become a more important criteria as women have gained economic independence. The desire for high marital satisfaction means that there is considerable positive pressure for people being married to make the marriage a priority. Whether they know it of not, couples make a decision about which criteria they will use to judge their marriage. This may change over time as well. At one stage of life, stability may seem very important. A couple with young children may value stability very highly, whereas, when the children are grown, quality and satisfaction may take on greater importance. One partner may be happy with a stable marriage that is low in quality and meeting few of their needs, whereas the other desires high quality or greater intimacy. The best of all possible worlds is reached when a couple finds all three - stability, quality and satisfaction to be high.

Financial
Responsibility

THE BIG SPENDER

A common pattern in marriage is that of the spender/saver: one partner is a careful saver, the other, a carefree spender. These roles often have a complementarity to them. The more one saves, the more the other spends. One keeps careful records of every cheque written, the other spends impulsively. These roles can feed each other, with the spender feeling hemmed in by the conservatism of the saver and responding by spending more. The spender might spend to "get even" with their cautious spouse, or simply to feel free. Based on this theory, someone who tends to be a spender, may actually become more restrained in a different relationship . . . their spending is partially a function of the dynamics of the relationship. There are those though, who by personality, are big spenders. Call it grandiosity, narcissism, or simply a boldness of spirit, they don't worry about spending or the debts they incur. Their "here and now" attitude towards life can be exhilarating, romantic and attractive . . . until it's your money they are spending. This is where the problem begins. As long as a big spender is only responsible for and to themselves, things go fine. When they are in a relationship, spending is apt to become a thorny issue. It is important for those of you who freely spend, to know the terror your spending creates in the hearts of those who love you.

**Your spending, which was a part of what attracted your
partner to you, could lead them to hate you.**

People who aren't big spenders usually like to feel in control. Your spending gives them that feeling of being pushed down the slide by a big kid when you were afraid to go. Your spending, which was a part of what attracted your partner to you, could lead them to hate you. It starts when they get concerned about your spending. Next they may make efforts to control you through jokes or sarcasm. If they don't reach you and get some behaviour change, they are likely to become resigned and give up on you or to become resentful. If you have the money to spend without getting into trouble with creditors, then it is your right to do it. You may however want to consider the temperament of your spouse and the goals that they have and their feelings about your spending style. The solution may be as simple as to be clear what the outside limits are on spending and to ensure that the reasonable concerns of your partner are addressed. Knowing what you have to "play with" outside of the common commitments of your marriage may make this side of your personality attractive once again. All that is required is the insight that what you consider safe and fun, might be scary and dangerous to the people you love.

THE BIG SAVER

aving money can be an important component of a healthy relationship . . . however, sometimes people get too much of a good thing. For instance, Nancy and Edwin are keen savers. At ages 23 and 27 they already own their own home and contribute to a retirement saving plan. Ed claims that if they keep up with the same rate of saving, they can retire at age 50. Every cent they make goes into the house or investments. Ed and Nancy are like many couples that fall in love and marry. When they began their relationship they spent lots of time together in pleasurable hours, going to shows and theatres, for leisurely dinners, on a beautiful honeymoon. They felt so secure in their love they didn't think they would miss the sacrifices needed to attain their financial goals. Their "all work and no play" policy began to damage the quality of their relationship. It began to lose the fun and playfulness that kept the relationship alive. It became a business relationship. Nancy attempted to get Ed to adjust the plan. Maybe it wasn't so important that they retire at 50. Maybe they needed to live now. Ed, the real saver of the two, became annoyed with Nancy. Nancy would propose a holiday. It would be too expensive.

Remember the adage "all work and no play makes Jack a dull boy!"

Edwin's myopia prevented him from noticing that his obstinacy and inflexibility was becoming a threat to the very relationship he was attempting to make secure. Ed needs to realize that a divorce would set his financial dreams back a lot further than the holiday Nancy proposed. If you are a "real saver" - if you don't know if you are, ask your friends and family; they'll let you know - then it should be important for you to find ways to moderate your conservatism. Remember the adage "all work and no play makes Jack a dull boy!" This could be you. Here is something you can try. Give yourself a budget for frivolous things. Then go to a mall and spend it on something you can't take home. An alternative would be to spend it on something non-functional for your spouse, like flowers, a painting, a bottle of perfume, a certificate for a massage. Practice supportive self talk, such as "This is what I work so hard for," "I deserve to have fun with my money," "Spend it now, it's no good to me when I'm dead." If you are a really conservative person, you likely have a fear of being out of control. Following this advice is not likely to turn you into a spend thrift. Relax, knowing you'll still keep your caution, but you won't alienate the people you love. Likely your money and your relationship will be protected.

THE EMOTIONAL MEANING OF MONEY

O ne of the important things for couples in the early stages of their relationship to do is to decide how to handle their finances. When having this kind of conversation, it is important to remember that money can have multiple emotional meanings. Money is an important symbol of personal autonomy. Ever since you had your first baby-sitting job or paper route, money meant that you had some control over your own destiny. As the relationship progresses, most people have a sense that they must begin to make joint financial decisions. How in your marriage can money continue to support a healthy feeling of independence? It is usually important that each spouse have some money they are solely responsible for, even if only so they can buy each other gifts without the other knowing exactly what they cost. It's important to respect personal autonomy within marriage. Security is another important emotional meaning of money. Without a certain solid income, one spouse may feel highly anxious. It's important to find a financial plan to looks after the primitive security needs of each partner while still leaving room to enjoy life a bit. If you find yourself arguing about money, it may be that you are really talking about what it takes for each of you to feel safe.

Whatever money means to you, it is important to assume that it will likely mean something different to your partner.

For some of us, money is a symbol of love, respect or worth. If you have money, you must be respectable and worthy. If you have less than your peers, then you should feel diminished. If you are really loved by your spouse, they will spend a lot of money on birthdays and special gifts. Money may mean loyalty to a family name. It is important when couples are planning about money, that they consider just what the money means to each partner. It's likely best to start with what money meant in your family of origin. If your parents were highly concerned about money, you likely internalized this value, or you may have rebelled against it. If your mother seemed trapped in an unhappy marriage, but had no independent money to command any power in the relationship, then you will likely insist on having financial autonomy. Whatever money means to you, it is important to assume that it will likely mean something different to your partner. When you hear your partner talk about their financial plans, ask yourself the question, "What is the emotional meaning of money to my partner?" Attempt to address the emotional issues beneath the financial ones, and you'll likely find it easier to reach an agreement on a financial plan that meets both your needs.

MAD MONEY

A common conflict among married couples is how to spend their money. Some partners in a flood of romantic intent, pool all of their funds and attempt to operate their financial lives from a common check book. For some it works. Others however, find themselves in predictable fights over control. The joint check book is a ready made situation for feelings of resentment and oppression. Every time she spends money that doesn't meet his standard, she feels his disapproval. This of course puts them into a father/daughter relationship dynamic that doesn't do them any good at all. If she complains about his purchases, or lack of keeping track, they develop a mother/son relationship which is just as damaging. An answer for many couples to these issues of control is Mad Money. Mad Money is discretionary money that each partner has at their disposal. They don't have to account for it or even tell their partner how they spent it. They can burn it, squander it on lottery tickets, invest it in high risk stocks, or stick it in a sock. It works this way. The couple decides just how much money they could afford for each other to have and yet still meet their common financial obligations and goals.

Mad money can help couples to side step a lot of unnecessary tension and maintain some of the joy of autonomous spending that shouldn't end with marriage.

It may be something like an allowance that each partner takes. If it is $5, $50 or $500, the key is that each person has equal mad money, and each refuses to comment on the way the other spends it. Mad money allows each partner to maintain some measure of financial autonomy. It allows a healthy separateness, necessary for a strong relationship. For couples where one person likes financial risks and the other is conservative, the answer is to figure out what their joint monthly needs are, and then determine how much each partner can contribute towards them. Let's say it costs them $2,000 per month to live. In a straightforward case, they each commit their first $1,000 of income to the home. Everything they make other than that is mad money. In this way, the conservative one isn't concerned that their freer spending mate will take risks with family assets, and the freer spending person is motivated to work harder to get the money they want to invest and take risks with. Whichever way couples arrange it, and for however much they determine, giving each partner in the relationship some discretionary spending ability is an important way to affirm individuality within the strength of a married relationship. Mad money can help couples to side step a lot of unnecessary tension and maintain some of the joy of autonomous spending that shouldn't end with marriage.

A BALANCED PORTFOLIO

Do we have enough money to get married? At times couples ask this question when the question that would be better asked is, "Do we have enough money to be married?" Money isn't everything, but a lack of it can add stress, discouragement and disappointment that is likely to detract from your marriage. Over the long haul, this can undermine feelings of love that brought you down the isle. But how much money is enough? Certainly this is all relative. It will depend on your own goals, hopes and expectations. It will owe a great deal to the experience of wealth in your family of origin. Each marriage partner will bring a bottom line of expectations that need satisfying. But what is realistic, reasonable and rational? Couples being married might want to ask themselves a series of questions. Is there enough for each of you to feel stable and secure? Is there enough for you to live in the "here and now" in a manner that is comfortable? Is there enough for each of you to be building a longer term security plan? Is there enough for some fun, adventure and maybe, children?

Money isn't everything, but it can make a big difference.

Couples are advised to consider the long term, their here and now needs as well as ensuring enough money for play. Some couples get their financial portfolio way out of balance in one of these areas. They may put everything into the long term future, forfeiting fun and adventure they need to keep their relationship fresh. Others indulge themselves too much in the hear and now and then find it extremely hard to adapt to the sacrifices of the child rearing stage. Some mistakenly believe they can be happy with less, only to find that as they age, their expectations increase. For example, when I was first married, my wife and I were both university students. For our first years of marriage we lived technically in poverty. It wasn't real poverty because we knew our educational time would satisfy our middle class needs and family backgrounds. If we were to be locked into that early lifestyle, frustration and disappointment would have had a heavy toll on our relationship. Money isn't everything, but it can make a big difference. Couples planning marriage need to ask, "Do we have the prospects to build a balanced financial portfolio that we both can be happy with?" If so, then maybe they can afford more than a wedding, but to be married as well.

PRENUPTIAL AGREEMENTS MAKE GOOD CENTS

The rise in remarried couples with children has renewed interest in establishing financial independence while being married. In the case of a 50 year old widow, wanting to insure that the estate she and her deceased husband accumulated would not go to her new husband and his children, a prenuptial agreement was a way to determine financial independence. It also makes sense for couples where one partner has considerable wealth before marriage. We've all read stories of the rich millionaire who falls in love with a fortune hunter. After a year of marriage she or he files for divorce and half the estate. The same prenuptial mechanism may also be a good precaution for "ordinary couples." A prenuptial agreement could exclude from common property such things as inheritances, heirlooms and debts, both issues that often become contentious when couples separate. Think of Susan. Her parents were killed in a car crash when she was 23. She had been married for one year at the time of their death. Six years later, her seven year marriage ended in a difficult divorce. Her husband, Chad, insisted that he be paid out one-half the value of the cottage Susan inherited from her parents.

**Given current marriage statistics, anyone embarrassed to discuss
a prenuptial agreement may be in an unhealthy state of denial
and suffer from basic unrealistic expectations.**

She may have had a legal case, but she wasn't in a financial position to challenge Chad. What was true of her family cottage could be true of other personal legacies such as cars, special furniture and jewellery. What about debts? Many people being married are worried about debts incurred by their fiancee but don't know what to do about it. In good faith, they may assume their spouse will take care of these. However, if they marry and divorce, how can they be sure the debt won't be split? Many people planning marriage avoid these issues, even though not dealing with them may cause anxiety for themselves and their extended family. And why? Perhaps because it seems bad taste to consider financial protection should the marriage fail, when it hasn't even begun. Every couple marrying needs to be realistic that strong stable marriages are not magically made. Almost any marriage can fail. Given current marriage statistics, anyone embarrassed to discuss a prenuptial agreement may be in an unhealthy state of denial and suffer from basic unrealistic expectations. A prenuptial agreement is a sign of realism, a way to preserve financial independence, reduce family anxiety and give evidence of a mature view of marriage. No marriage is guaranteed. The best insurance is realism and effort.

My Love Affair With Money

Although couples often have conflict over matters related to money, seldom do they really take the time to understand where and how their partner's views about money have developed. Actually, few people take the time to understand themselves when it comes to their relationship with money. Olivia Mellan, writing in the March/April 1992 edition of *The Family Therapy Networker*, has offered a solution. It begins with asking yourself about the way that money has played a role in your family down through the decades. Start with your grandparents. Was money bountiful and a gateway to pleasure? Perhaps your grandparents were affected by the great depression? Where there reversals of fortune, with someone losing a business and then experiencing depression and social shame? Was it a story of immigrants who struggled hard for every penny and thus guarded it jealously? Did your parents worry about money? Fight about money? Feel controlled by a lack of money? In my family of origin, there were two very different orientations to money. My mother came from the right side of the tracks, where money was plentiful. They weren't rich, but they enjoyed all the amenities society had to offer at that time. My father came from the poor side of town.

Imagine that money is a person with whom you are having a relationship. Write to money describing how you feel about them and how you think the relationship is going thus far.

His father was unemployed during the depression. This was a source of shame. He had a chronically ill sister at a time before medicare made medicine accessible for all. My parents' experience of money shaped very different attitudes towards it, which in turn helped to shape mine. Mellan suggests that each person, having done their family "money genogram" write out a "money monologue." Imagine that money is a person with whom you are having a relationship. Write to money describing how you feel about them and how you think the relationship is going thus far. A person who has come from a family with an anxious relationship about money might write "I love you so much I want to be with you every minute of every day. Thoughts of you consume my mind. I know I hold you too close and that it shuts others out. It seems I can't help myself. When you aren't around I feel lonely and insecure." Each person's monologue with money will be different. Once you have written about your dialogue with money, write down what you think your mother, your father and your God (or your Higher Power) would think about your relationship with money. When the entire exercise is complete, ask yourself, what have I learned about my affair with money? Do you need to be less possessive and obsessive? Perhaps you have been neglectful, careless or inconsistent? Share your insights with your partner and see what you can learn.

MONEY POLARITIES

Although there may be some ways of relating to money which can be considered unhealthy, for the most part, it is simply the differences in approach between marital partners that cause the problems. If one partner is a compulsive gambler, this could likely be considered unhealthy by most people. Likewise, if someone hoards their money even though they have lots, this also could be seen as pathological. Differences between most partners in relation to money are usually not this dramatic. A person with a conscientious personality style will likely be interested in planning. They want to budget for everything. Two people with this personality style will likely get along very well. Match a conscientious style of person with a dramatic or mercurial personality style, and you get instant money problems. The passionate personality styles will feel hemmed in by planning. Unconsciously they may have been drawn to someone with this personality style sensing that they would be a balance or touch stone. Consciously, however, they will struggle against the schemes of the planner. Those with a self-confident streak will see money as something that brings pleasure and ego enhancement. They will want the best clothes, an attractive house, furnishings that make a statement. If they can't afford it, they would borrow with a sense of entitlement.

**Money polarities are neither good nor bad.
They simply need to be understood.**

If they were paired with a vigilant personality styled partner, someone interested in control with a low threat threshold, this partner would likely feel that the personal spending of their partner was done "against them" or to spite them. A devoted, home oriented, introverted partner might be contented with much less: a more modest home, cars, clothes and furnishings within their means and no borrowing. It is important in understanding the polarities between couples in regards to money, to know something of their personality structure and family background with money. Think about your partner. Do they tend towards those personality styles that are extroverted and impulsive? You can expect that they will handle money in similar ways. Does your partner tend towards those personality characteristics that are introverted, interested more in family than friends, wanting to be in control in their own little world? You can expect that they will likely be very conservative and even possessive with money. When my parents call long distance, dad gets to the point and mother rambles. I feel anxious talking with him, because I think he is thinking about the cost, but I also enjoy the calls. These attitudes are a part of the polarity within me and between them. Money polarities are neither good nor bad. They simply need to be understood and solutions negotiated for each person to develop a healthy relationship with money and their partner.

ROMANCE & FINANCIAL RESPONSIBILITY

What's the best predictor of the future? The past. Want to know what the best indicators are of your partner's performance as a mate? Their family of origin. Now, put these two together, and what do you learn about how your partner might behave as a money manager: look at their past record with money and the way money was handled in their family of origin. Consider John and Ellen's story. When they courted, John was the most romantic of suitors. He seemed to have a flare for the dramatic, including money spent on expensive gifts, dinners at the best restaurants, flowers for special occasions. Ellen assumed that if money was not a problem for these frills, then money wasn't a problem. What she didn't know was that John was a person who liked to pursue, to have a good front, but that his credit cards were often at their limit and his account, overdrawn. Ellen had grown up in a home where money was scarce and carefully spent. She had learned to assume that people would not buy what they couldn't afford. Because the things John bought seemed extravagant, there was an air of excitement so different from her family of origin. It wasn't until she was engaged to John that she began to suspect his chaotic financial situation, and not until she was married that she found out how bad it really was. This was a major disillusionment to Ellen.

Without financial responsibility, the romance will likely die.

On the other hand, John didn't understand Ellen's disillusionment. He had been raised in a family where money was impulsively spent. There was not moral judgement associated with spending or saving money, other than that money meant there was a good time now. To complicate matters, John was the baby in his family. Like the baby in the cartoon television series, *Dinosaurs*, John's implied motto was "Gotta Love Me." In this situation, John lived for romance and knew how to create it. Ellen was starved for romance and was vulnerable and naive in face of the excitement. Responsibility was not important to John. To Ellen, responsibility was the assumed starting point. John and Ellen's story tells us several important things about money in marriage. One is, that without financial responsibility, the romance will likely die. On the other hand, money can help to create romance. Thirdly, it is important for intimate partners to know something of their partner's financial and family past to understand and predict how they might handle financial responsibilities in the future. With communication and cooperation, courage and negotiation, things could be different for the John and Ellen's of the world.

WHO'S RESPONSIBLE

Culture has assigned certain roles to marriage partners. Despite the fact that these may be politically incorrect, some of them still carry a lot of weight. One such set of roles is that men are responsible for earning the money and women love to spend it. Sometimes though, this dynamic is the other way around in relationships. The important point is, often issues of responsibility, control and independence are crystallized around these financial roles. Think of how you feel about the way that your partner handles money. If you feel some annoyance, fear or resentment, then it is likely that you have a problem as a couple. Very often, financial problems begin with mild feelings, such as being concerned that your partner spends too freely, or conversely, that your partner is too cheap. If you feel annoyance with your partner's money management, it may be that you feel that they are taking control away from you or that they may be attempting to dominate you. Your feelings can be an important index of how your financial affairs are being run. If you have any of these feelings, it may be important to do some major reflection on the way money is handled in your relationship, with some of the suggestions offered below:

1. **It is important to develop language and attitudes that express the "we" ness of the relationship. Whatever plans you make, there should be a sense that "we made these plans because they fit for us."**
2. **It is important to have shared decision making about the major direction of your financial life. This means working towards agreement on how much money to save, spend and play with.**
3. **Agreement should be reached on who has the responsibility to pay bills, to save and how much money each of you has as mad money.**
4. **Contingency plans should be made, so that if your financial situation changes, you will have already thought through some of the implications for your relationship and how you would block negative consequences. People get laid off, business down turns, workers go on strike, and sickness and inflation can affect even the best of plans.**

In times of stress, we tend to regress to what we learned in our family of origin. How can your plans protective you from falling instinctively in patterns that may destroy the sense of "we" ness that can be achieved through good joint planning? Money in marriage is a shared responsibility. Planning is the process through which you insure your financial management builds your sense of companionship.

Equalitarian Roles

THE EQUALITARIAN RELATIONSHIP

Equalitarian relationships. Hear the words and you know what it means. Yet once I had an argument with a school teacher friend, who said, equalitarian isn't a word. He said, "you must mean egalitarian." I checked the dictionary of the day, and found out that my friend was right: equalitarian wasn't a dictionary word. Nonetheless, it is a word that has been used in family social science for some time. Equalitarian seems to be similar to egalitarian. Egalitarian, however, reminds me of my history lessons on the French revolution. It connotes equality between classes of persons. Equalitarian has meaning directed towards shared responsibilities, such as in family household management. It is a word that speaks to the relationships between men and women in families. Another word that bears a close relationship to equalitarian is feminist. My understanding of feminism is that it applies to someone who believes that men and women should have equal opportunities, rights and obligations. In equalitarian marriages, men and women share equally. There are no assumptions that men take out the garbage, women do the dishes; men go to work, women mind the children; women write the letters to relatives, men make the sexual overtures.

**Equalitarian relationships should be seen as
something to aspire towards.**

It is assumed the men are capable of doing dishes, writing letters and minding children, just as women are able to go to work, take out the garbage and make sexual overtures. Discrimination and distinction are not made on the basis of sex, but on personality instead. Within equalitarian relationships, there is a complete sharing of relationship responsibilities. Household chores, financial management, child rearing and nurturing the emotional health of the relationship are duties for which each partner feels an obligation. Equalitarian relationships are a shift from marriages built on gender based role complementarity. Remember "Leave it to Beaver" or "Happy Days?" These 1950's families represent gender based complementarity. The unfortunate part about a lot of these marriages was that certain aspects of human personality were trapped within rigid role definitions. Men who may have been great cooks weren't allowed inside a kitchen . . . they could barbecue, but that was about it. Women who could fix cars often weren't even expected to drive them if a man was around. Equalitarian marriages reflect a new idea of sharing in marriage. There can be complementarity, with one spouse taking on a lead role in certain tasks, such as handling money, or nurturing children. The distinguishing point between the complementarity of the 1950's and the equalitarian marriage is that in the latter, differences are based on skills and personality, rather than on gender. As such, equalitarian relationships should be seen as something to aspire towards, since they hold the promise of each spouse fulfilling his or her potential within the marriage.

SEEING EACH OTHER BEAUTIFUL

The movie *A River Runs Through It* tells the tale of a brotherhood bond- two sons of a preacher growing up in the beauty of the Montana countryside. The script must have been written by an Adlerian psychologist, because the brothers fit the traditional portraits of oldest and youngest same sex siblings. Big brother chooses a career path that pleases his father; he is stolid and cautious. Younger brother is a romantic character who defies the rules. As the older says of the younger, "He was an artist, who transcended time and space." In the end, the younger brother defies the rules of the wrong people and is murdered, presumably for his unpaid gambling debts. The story is narrated from the perspective of the older brother. He says that after his brother's death his father asked him many times what he knew of his younger brother. Though the murdered son was the antithesis of his staid Presbyterian preacher father, the father said to the older son, "You knew more than that about him; you knew he was beautiful." That line, "You knew he was beautiful" reminded me of the words of a young woman in the play *The Rainmaker*. The rainmaker was a person of dreams, a person for whom ideas were always more tantalizing than reality. "Nothing is quite as real as when it is in your head." A young woman offers him a different perspective. She says that at times she looks at her father as if for the first time. Then she sees things about him that she never noticed before ... little mannerisms and movements. She says, "Then I love him so much, I could cry, and I thank God I took time to see him real."

Is it time for you to take a second look at someone in your life?

The view of the father in *A River Runs Through It* and the young woman in *The Rainmaker* could be described as a belief that there is something beautiful and divine within life itself. When we study people, we see growth and change at many levels, a tapestry of paradoxes midst a variety of personality styles. As well known family therapist Michael White would say, this is a process of "exotizing the familiar." There are those who take the impoverished view that familiarity breeds contempt - that love must fall victim to time and proximity. They believe that as couples live together that they should come to find each other less intriguing. This has to be recognized for what it is: a very limited, negative view of life that leads to perpetual discontent. What would one expect for a marriage where those being married held this view? These are the people who are bound to become cynical. But there is another way. We can start with the idea that every human being is beautiful. Each one is struggling to meet his or her needs and fulfil their personal dreams. If we can detach from a significant other enough to see them "real" and beautiful, then familiarity can deepen and enrich marriage. Is it time for you to take a second look at someone in your life?

WHAT A WOMAN WANTS FROM A MAN

I might be the least qualified person to write about this topic. For several years I was a clinical supervisor of a group of graduate university students preparing for professional counselling careers. There was so much demand for the program that I was asked to take seven rather than the usual six persons for a full team. The unique feature of this team was the gender - they were all women. Since it was a marriage and family therapy team, we spent a lot of time reflecting on the hopes that men and women have for their relationships. As supervisor, I was not shy about offering my views, particularly those about what a man needs to do in order to keep a woman happy. Then came Christmas. My gift from the team was a little book entitled *Everything Men Know about Women*. Sound like a good title? Yes! However, the pages of the book are absolutely blank, sending an important message, "Men know nothing about women." I got the point. Since then I have listened carefully. Although I will never again presume to pontificate on what women want of men, I can offer what I have learned as I have asked this question of various women. One lesson comes from my experience in post-divorce counselling. A woman whose first marriage dissolved when her husband fell in love with another woman was telling me about the difference between her first marriage and the relationship she has with the man she currently lives with. She said, "I used to spend my time doing things for my husband; now I spend time doing things *with* my partner." Doing *for* or doing *with* - this is a significant difference for many women.

"Someone to care about them, to pay attention to them" - and then, after a pause, "and to create some magic."

They report that they want a companion, they don't want to be the "maid," the "mother," the "cook." Although they may be willing to fill some of these roles, they want to share many of their free time activities along *with* their partner. When I asked a female colleague "What does a woman want from a man?", she said without thinking, "Someone to care about them, to pay attention to them" - and then, after a pause, "and to create some magic." These seem like simple things to do, yet she says that men are often so self-centred in relationships, they seldom have room to consider what their spouse thinks and feels. But what about the "magic?" Part of it seems to be created by the doing *with*, the caring for and paying attention to. The other part seems to have to do with paying attention to the need for change, stimulation, adventure, romance. The popular mother/ daughter country western singing team, The Judds, have a song called "Baby's Got the Blues" in which they sing a line "Women need men to make them feel alive." What I think this means is to create the conditions of humour, levity, and newness, to do things out of the ordinary, to grow together. When considered, it seems like a do-able list, something within the reach of every man.

THE FEAR OF WHAT WE MOST WANT

In his excellent book on parenting, *Compassionate Child-Rearing*, Robert Firestone discusses the importance of a strong couple bond. Loving and in-love parents, who treat each other with dignity and respect, provide an environment in which children flourish. He goes on to say that although parents will claim that they love their children, if one were to analyze their family interactions, one would see that often parents are rude, belittling, controlling, and demanding. Their communication with their children is laced with interruptions, sarcasm, put downs and poor listening. The outside observer, watching a parent chastise a child in a grocery store, feels almost embarrassed at the incongruity. Often poor parenting emerges from parents whose own emotional hungers are not being met in their adult relationships. Firestone asserts that many parents do not get their needs met because they are afraid of intimacy. To really be in love means that we might feel vulnerable and dependent. Firestone writes, "Most people, I believe, are intolerant, on a deep level, of being loved, admired, and personally prized for their unique qualities. Fear of loss or abandonment, dread of being rejected, the poignancy and sadness evoked by the positive emotions of tenderness and love themselves, eventually become intolerable, particularly for those men and women who suffered from lack of love and affectionate contacts in childhood." This means that we develop ways to stop ourselves from getting what we most want. If it sounds irrational, that's because it is irrational . . . but it is very human.

**We develop ways of creating distance, preferring safety
over the scary exhilaration of openness and love.**

Falling out of love is emotionally safer for many than the challenge of continued openness. Maybe this is what people mean when they say that couples should "work" at a marriage - challenging the invisible, irrational, yet very real intimacy boundaries we create to limit what we most want. How does it happen? There is the man who procrastinates when it comes to doing fun things with his wife . . . he allows her to do all the initiating, even though he knows she wants to be romanced. Likely he holds his feelings in, stops sharing his heart-felt secrets, refuses to cry even when he feels threatened or sad. He chooses work over her and then doesn't explain the compulsion he has to be successful and how it conflicts with his desire to meet her needs. For her part, she may confide more secrets to her friends than her spouse, hold back sexually, and no longer ask for what she needs, prejudging his responses. They might talk about each other to their friends in sarcastic or derogatory ways. They might tease in a way that creates distance and hurt. Whatever they do, the aim is always the same, to find safety at the expense of intimacy. But does it have to be this way? That's up to you!

LEISURE'S CHALLENGE TO MARRIAGE

The economic structure of our society has changed drastically in the past 50 years. This change has brought new challenges for intimate relationships, as in the case of the use of leisure time. In my grandfather's day, work meant six days a week, eight hours a day. My father owned his own business, and worked five and one half days a week, a reduction from his father's era. Two weeks was considered a good annual vacation. Today, many of us think of a normal work week as five days, seven hours a day, for thirty-five hours. Three weeks annual vacation is considered a minimum, along with numerous statutory holidays, not known in grandfather's day. Although there are many people who work more than these hours, there is clearly a difference in expectation, from my grandfather's day, to today. When he wasn't at work, maintaining a home represented a much larger time commitment than it does for us. He had to get up in the morning and feed coal into the fire; he didn't have a car so he had to build-in time to walk to work, the store, the church, the relatives. I can still remember grandmother's washing machine with the rollers for squeezing the water out before she hung them to dry. Today a machine spins the moisture out before we throw them into the dryer. There was no such thing as fast food, and gardening was a necessity, not a hobby.

If we can use this leisure time well, then marriages can become more than partnerships in survival, they can become friendships.

One would think that having more leisure time was an automatic advantage for relationships, but not necessarily so. In fact, what has happened is that this greater amount of disposable time has lead to a shift from an interest in marital adjustment to a focus on marital satisfaction. When a greater portion of life is taken up with the tasks associated with survival, then stability, predictability and compatibility around household management seem to be the key features of a so called "good marriage." When simple survival is less an issue, the quality of life begins to take on more importance. The question is no longer, "Will we survive?" but, "Will we enjoy ourselves while we are surviving?" I have heard those who are bewildered by the high divorce rates of today blame this on the quality of people and their commitment. It isn't that people are different in marriage today; it is that the surrounding context has changed dramatically. This has placed a new demand on marriage, which carries an implicit opportunity. If we can use this leisure time well, then marriages can become more than partnerships in survival; they can become friendships. Friendships sometimes grow out of struggle for survival, but where this struggle does not exist, a new challenge is presented. Communicating well and bonding through leisure time have become the imperatives for marriage in a new economic climate.

MAKING TWO CAREERS WORK

T hat the number of women working outside of the home is growing is likely no surprise. This well documented statistical trend has been accompanied by an attitude shift which you could notice in my opening line. Instead of saying, "the number of women *working* is growing," I said, "the number of women *working outside the home* is growing." The assumption here is that women at home, work. In fact, studies tend to show that women who work outside of the home have a second full time job, household management. As women take up responsibilities in the outside world, there has not been a correspondingly large shift in men taking up work at home. What effect does a woman working outside the home have on a marital relationship? Some proponents of the so-called "traditional family" believe that it is bound to have a negative effect; however, recent research does not support this. In a study reported in the May 1992 edition of *Journal of Marriage and the Family,* sociologists from the University of Cincinnati and the State University of New York report that the effect of a woman working depends on the gender role identities and role expectations of the particular marital partners. In other words, the couple's attitude determined whether or not the fact of women working would have a negative impact on the marriage.

Regardless of the employment status of the wife, the more sensitive husbands were, the more positive the marriage.

The researchers went further, and looked at the question of the impact on marriage where women break through the "glass ceiling" and become more successful than their husbands. In these cases, where a woman may have a higher status profession than her spouse, if her husband is *sensitive* to and *supportive* of her career, then marital quality will be high. The research also supported the conclusion that what the husband thinks about the woman working is more important to the experience of marital quality for both spouses than are the attitudes of the woman. An interesting side line to the study was that where women were married to men of high status positions, the more traditional the man's views, the more negatively their wives viewed the relationship. Regardless of the employment status of the wife, the more sensitive husbands were, the more positive the marriage. The upshot of the finding is that it is not whether or not women work during marriage that counts; it is whether or not the couple, and the men in particular, have attitudes that support the idea of the woman working. Much of the responsibility seems to fall back to the man. If he can be supportive and sensitive, his wife will likely be happy, working or not working. Men need to back their sensitivity and support up with instrumental help. This means insuring that if she works, that he finds some way to lighten her load at home. Dual careerism is not a problem to marriage; it is our attitudes and the slowness of men to see the family revolution around them that hurts marital quality.

97

EQUALITY = FULFILLED POTENTIAL

A developmental psychologist named Eric Erickson described the majors stages we go through in life. One near the end is called "generativity vs despair." In this stage of later life, a person either has a sense that they have done something worthwhile, or they despair that they have missed their opportunities, usually becoming cynical and bitter. What can be more depressing than to feel that you have fulfilled only a part of your potential? Yet that is the situation culturally proscribed roles have placed many women in. Culture has also ascribed roles to men, but I don't believe it has ever been as restrictive as it has been for women. As well, men may be more oblivious to their constraints, and, as the saying goes, "ignorance is bliss." Many men have not realized that the role of provider has often discouraged them being sensitive nurturers. Equalitarian marriages are based on the premise that each partner should bring to the marriage the strengths indigenous to their personality. When I was in graduate school I took a course, as do all psychologists, in psychological measurement. Remember those aptitude tests you took in high school or college? It has been my practice to try these kinds of tests out on my own family. I administered a test of spatial relations to my wife. This test can show that a person has an aptitude for engineering. To my surprise, my wife scored in the 99th percentile.

Each person does what they are best at and which they enjoy.

That means that only 1% of the population would be more likely to be successful in this area. I applied the test to other members of her family and found that they were uniformly high in this aptitude. When I administered the test to myself, I was in the bottom 25%, along with the criminally insane. These test results released something in our marriage. I had been valiantly trying to play the male role of doing all the "fix it" things. If there was a renovation to be planned or repair to be carried out, I'd have done the work, despite being horribly frustrated, while usually messing it up. If there was a tradesman to talk to, I'd do the talking. Meanwhile, my wife was busy with dishes, cleaning, ironing and the wash. The test results made me realize that we were mismatched for our roles. Now she talks to the tradesmen, does the plumbing and plans the renovations. If there is something mechanical that needs fixing, I give it to her, and then I go off to do the dishes. I love ironing. I find it relaxing and it gives me a sense of accomplishment. I never get frustrated with it, like I used to with things that don't work. I'm also a bit of neat freak, so I get a bang out of tidying things up. There are times I feel a bit wimpy about the way our roles are assigned. I have to remind myself that we have worked out a logical system. Each person does what they are best at and which they enjoy. In this way, gender does not block our potential.

A MESSAGE FOR MEN

Over the course of a lifetime, those things that are meaningful to us seem to change. When you were a child, a new toy could mean the world. In high school, waking up without pimples would be a joy. The rewards of marriage also change throughout the course of life. In the earliest stage of relationships, roses, interesting dates, the stuff of which romance is made, can make a big difference. Usually these little gifts lose their impact once the relationship advances to the point where the couple is living together. At this point, the issue of fairness in household management begins to take on greater importance. A typical case is Bonnie. She and her husband Tom have one small child. Both had come from traditional families where their mothers had been responsible for the majority of household functions. Bonnie and Tom both work outside the home full time. When they first married they continued on the patterns of their parents. Bonnie did the cooking, cleaning, shopping and laundry, as well as working full time. Tom would work full time, spend time with his friends, play in a hockey league and fix the car when necessary. When their first child was born, Tom continued his life style, while Bonnie incorporated all of the laborious tasks associated with child rearing into her already busy regimen of work and household management. She didn't understand why she was feeling resentment towards Tom, why she didn't feel as sexually attracted towards him, and why she felt so lonely.

**It is important for men to know how to be sensitive,
to listen to feelings, and to be romantic.**

Tom didn't wake up to the changes happening in their marriage either. Instead, he felt rejected by her decreased interest in marriage. Overall, their marital satisfaction took a distinct dive. What Tom needs to realize is that *instrumental* helping, at this stage of the relationship, would make all the difference in the world. It is important for men to know how to be sensitive, to listen to feelings, and to be romantic. But during the early stages, when the couple is adjusting to living together, it is important for the man to take the initiative to insure that their is equality in the division of labour. This is the bread and butter of respect and caring within relationships. If the kind of gross unfairness evident in Tom and Bonnie's marriage is not corrected, the outcome is predictable. A man interested in the long term welfare of his marriage needs to have a healthy self-interest in seeing that he is carrying half the chores. I find that men still tend to think that their work outside of the home is their primary contribution today, despite the so-called women's liberation movement. This type of thinking gives men some privileges in marriage, but in the long run, leads to an alienation in love. Men have a choice. Do they want the privileges of the past, or do they want to protect the basis for love? I would contend that the latter is in their best interest.

POWER AND CONTROL

One of the benefits of the women's liberation movement has been a trend towards equality in family relations. This has lead to a change in power differentials within marriage. Ask anyone within the shelter movement for battered women, and they will tell you that male/female relationships are coloured more by issues of power and control, than by love. Consider the man whose wife has left him and checked into a shelter for abused women. Her husband is finally able to contact her and he proposes his undying love. Question: is it love he feels, or a desire to be in control? Is this her best interest he aspires towards, or the contentment of winning a competition? Is he broken up because he regrets his actions and wishes to share his life with her, changing his behaviour, or is he simply a bad loser? There have been changes within the legal field which recognize the power and control issues between men and women. Actually, it may be more accurate to say the power and control issues of men in relation to women, since men seem to have a greater interest in control. Nowadays, in many jurisdictions there is no longer a law against "rape." Rape is now known as "sexual assault." This suggests a shift from a "sexual crime" to a crime of power. Hopefully, this sounds repugnant to you, since we believe in a value of individual freedom. In a democracy, no person should be dominated by another. When this occurs, slavery emerges.

Marriages between unequals can survive and have qualities of comfort and love, but they will never match the relationship of equals.

There are still vestiges of this old culture embedded within the new. Many women still expect men to take the lead and be the person who is in control. Many women still organize their lives around men, moving when their husband chooses to, waiting for him to come home, waiting for him to call. This kind of dependency is evidence of a power differential that leaves the woman in a lesser position and it is understandable that many men would rather not change this pattern. The relationship, however, can no longer be a relationship of equals. The cost: inequality erodes the intensity of love, which can only be found between two equals. Couples can have complementarity in marriage and still have equality, as long as the complementarity is not based on gender differences . . . Positive complementarity is based on different talents, with neither partner feeling less powerful than the other. Marriages between unequals can survive and have qualities of comfort and love, but they will never match the relationship of equals. This is why couples who truly seek a "love marriage" need to be sure that where power and control are concerned, each partner feels like an equal. Neither is dependent on the other. In this way, marriage is more an institution of love and choice, rather than obligation and duty.

LEISURE TIME

Does absence make the heart grow fonder? Do happy couples spend more time together? Does spending time together lead to a happier marriage? Is there a circular, reciprocal relationship between time spent together, and marital happiness? These were some of the questions researchers explored in a three wave study involving members of 1,300 couples sampled over an eight year period of marriage. Members of these couples were interviewed in 1980, 1983 and again in 1988. Each time they completed questions having to do with the amount of time they spent together and with how happy they were with their relationship. A first interesting finding was that there was no difference in the way men and women reported about these two variables. Second, couples who were happier with their relationship tended to be those couples who spent more time together. This supports the idea that there is a general circular link between couples spending time together and being happy. Happiness and time together seem to feed on each other. But which comes first, the chicken or the egg? Although time together and happiness are closely linked, it seems that being happily married is a greater guarantee that the process will get going.

It is possible to spend time together and not be happily married, but in most cases, people who are happily married make time for each other.

The relationship between time spent together and marital happiness does change throughout the stages of the couples life, however. Time together is dramatically impacted by the presence of children in the family. The research found that the immediate effects of children being introduced into the family were negative for the relationship, but in the long run, their presence was a positive influence on time spent together and marital happiness. The findings of this study suggest that people in relationships who never seem to find time for each other and the relationship, may in fact be making a serious negative comment on the state of their marriage. Certainly there may be some couples at some times in their life, that are pulled by outside commitments that make it very difficult for them to spend time together. This is particularly so when young children or elderly parents require care, or when a new business venture or career is being launched. In these cases, the marital partners may yearn to have more time with one another, but have disciplined themselves to forgo this for a period of time. A prolonged pattern of limited marital interaction likely means there isn't much of a marriage. They become roommates, more than spouses. For example, some people think that if their mate didn't work so much, the marriage may be happier, but it may also be, that the "work-a-holic" spouse actually works so much because there is nothing for them at home. Time spent together appears to be a quick litmus test of a marriage, something that people interested in strong marriages need to pay attention to.

Children
&
Parenting

THE CHOICE ABOUT CHILDREN

T here was a time when getting married implied having children. This is no longer true, particularly since many marrying couples are older and entering a second relationship. They may already have children from a first relationship. What kind of factors go into the decision making regarding having children? As is so often the case, despite our more "open" society, couples frequently skirt discussing these important questions, and understandably so - the decision is fraught with strong emotional attachments. Consider the case of the couple who are marrying where one has children, and the other does not. The one who does not have children of his or her own may hold a secret longing to have biological offspring. This implies that the partner, who already has children, might not have the same desire . . . after all, they've done that already. It may be that they really want to have children with their new partner, but they may not be as keen. If they do proceed to have children, the one who has been through it all before seems like the expert . . . but their expertise is sometimes not appreciated, for it reminds the partner who has never experienced childbirth, about their partner's previous marriage. The situation is ripe for an unconscious kind of one-up-man-ship. Then there is money. For most two income couples, having children represents an increase in expenditures and a major drop in cash flow.

The implication is that couples contemplating marriage
should discuss the ramifications of having children.

How does this fit with the financial goals of the couple? Who is keenest about having the child? Who hopes the most to build the financial portfolio? Will one partner be hurt if the other partner is concerned about money? If they aren't compatible, how can this be resolved without hurt, hidden obligations and resentment? Conceiving children represents such an enormous commitment that if it is taken on half-heartedly by one partner, the other is bound to feel abandoned. This will likely have implications for how the children are raised and the kind of love between the partners. I have met many divorcing people who have told me that a critical incident in their loss of love happened in relationship to having their children. Either the spouse was unavailable when the baby was born, didn't come to the hospital enough, didn't seem interested enough, or was preoccupied with the financial costs. These behaviours are often experienced as an unforgivable injury to the love dynamic in the relationship. The implication is that couples contemplating marriage should discuss the ramifications of having children. It is important to use one's very best communication skills, and particularly on this matter, not to try to get one's way. It is best to explore each other's feelings, then the surrounding issues. Watch out for making assumptions, particularly that your partner's feelings don't change over time, because they will.

REPRODUCTIVE CHOICE

One day in my practice of family therapy I decided to ask each scheduled couple if they had any concerns related to reproductive choice. It didn't just come to me out of the blue. I'd been working with a couple the evening before, where the woman had a tremendous fear of being pregnant again. This fear had been inhibiting their sexual relationship and this in turn was affecting other aspects of their marriage. To my surprise, five out of five couples that day had some form of issue around reproductive choice. There was the man who was procrastinating on a joint couple decision, in which he had promised to obtain a vasectomy. There was the woman who wanted to have another child and her husband did not. He felt that she was not being responsible about taking her birth control pills, so he was reluctant to approach her for sex. He thought that she was attempting to trick him into fathering another child. There was the woman who was attempting to establish a new career, a career that her husband did not whole-heartedly support. In this case, she at times thought that he secretly hoped to impregnate her so as to frustrate her career plans. And then there was the couple where there was no practical contraception which seemed acceptable for the wife as the husband did not like to wear a condom. These concerns complicate an already sensitive issue. I have since found that reproductive issues such as these are common among fertile couples.

Often partners will discuss reproduction at one point in their relationship, and falsely assume that this view has stayed the same.

It is easy to focus on what is secondary by getting caught up with the reproductive concern. As with most couple issues, however, it is not what appears on the surface that is most important. The key is for the partners to pay attention to the *feelings* associated with these problems. The spouse most concerned about pregnancy will likely believe that his or her partner is attempting to gain control through reproduction. This could lead to anger, resentment, distrust and a feeling of being alone. A first step in this reproductive discussion would be to explore the feelings of each spouse about their current reproductive status. The spouse who has been slow in obtaining a vasectomy may have some genuine fears that need to be acknowledged and overcome before he can defeat procrastination. The spouse worried about being tricked into fathering another child may require practical reassurance. If we were to continue the focus on feelings, we would have to ask, "How does the spouse feel, whose husband says he sometimes worries that she would trick him into a pregnancy?" She may feel insulted, hurt, falsely accused. If these feelings about the issue cannot be understood, acknowledged, and then put aside, there will be little progress in these discussions that are so important to the success of every couple.

Do Children Ruin a Marriage?

Studies of marital dissolution have given child-bearing bad press. They have suggested that having children leads to marital problems. This was sometimes expressed as the curvilinear hypothesis. Imagine a simple graph. Marital satisfaction is recorded from low to high going up the side of this graph. Length of marriage is written along the bottom. If people were happy when they married, and stayed that way throughout their lives, the graph would show a straight line running across the top. If all marriage started great and gradually deteriorated, the graph would show a line starting at the top left hand corner, cutting the graph into two triangles, indicating low marital satisfaction later in marriage. The curvilinear hypothesis was that the line on the graph would look like a big U, with marital satisfaction being high in the early years, low during the children rearing years and then steadily increasing in the empty nest stage. Recently however, social scientists have been saying that low marital satisfaction during the child rearing years may not be a function of children, but really the function of keeping love alive as the relationship matures. As relationships wear on, they tend to reach the "blah - stage" children or no children. In fact, in many relationships, having children decreases the importance of marital satisfaction. Having children can add such excitement to a relationship, that marital satisfaction becomes less important.

Having children *changes* a marriage.

Studies, though, are indicating that more couples are choosing childlessness. It may be that there are unrealistic views about the stresses of parenting and the subsequent effect on marriage. A study of 600 couples in the early years of marriage found that a growing number of couples thought that having children would interfere with their economic and recreational pursuits. The major advantage of having children was thought to derive from seeing them as necessary for having a "real" family life where they were considered to be a source of love and affection. Couples rated having children as only slightly more valuable than having extra money or having a neat and orderly household or finding new interests and hobbies. More than half the 600 couples reported that freedom of movement, leisure time and having free time with one's spouse were more important than having children. Given these types of values, having children likely will be a strain for many couples: there *will* be a loss of quality time for each other, a restriction of freedom of movement, less chance of having extra money, and the house won't be as tidy. It would not be fair to say, however, that having children disrupts and ruins a marriage. Having children *changes* a marriage. Children present a test of the maturing and flexibility of the adult individuals in the marriage and of the marriage relationship itself.

PREDICTING A GOOD PARENT

Parenting styles can have a significant impact on marital relationships, as people who teach parenting classes know full well. A common phenomena in parent education classes is that only one parent will attend the class. Usually they will learn some exciting new ideas that can make a significant impact on the well being of their children. They rush home to tell their spouse, only to receive a cool reception. At times, the keener the one taking the classes, the less receptive their spouse becomes. Maybe you've had this experience yourself. What happens next, is the one with the new knowledge attempts to apply it. This might lead to some teasing or sarcasm. In turn, the one with new knowledge begins to analyze their partner's parenting practices. Any habits that don't fit with the new knowledge will begin to be a thorn in the side. A loss of respect ensues which damages the fragile love bond. For this reason, leaders of parenting classes encourage couples to attend together, so they begin to apply new skills simultaneously. When reasonably well-functioning people have children, the spouse is usually considered less important than the child. If one was forced to make a choice between their spouse or their child, most would choose the child. In this type of emotional triangle, bad parenting is like interfering with the cub of a mother bear.

The best predictor of future behaviour, is the past.
It is important to understand whether or not your
partner received quality parenting themselves.

Good fathering is a particularly important variable in maintaining relationship quality. Usually, if a woman does not think her husband is doing a good job of fathering, this will lead to a loss of respect - a basic condition of long term love. Is there a way to tell who will be a good parent? Certainly this is a question that anyone entering marriage should reflect on, particularly those who expect to have children one day. The best predictor of future behaviour is the past. It is important to understand whether or not your partner received quality parenting themselves. Did his or her parents meet all their needs? Was there respect for the child? How was discipline handled? Was it consistent and sensible, or erratic and punitive? This rule about the past predicting the future does have limitations. Many people who received poor parenting resolve to do things differently. However, it is not what they *say* they want to do for their kids in the future, but what they have actually *done* to acquire better relationship skills and how well they use those skills in the present. It is truly important for any person considering marriage to know they are not only choosing a mate, they may also be choosing a parent for their children.

THERE ARE NO EXPERTS AT HOME

While out for a walk, my wife stopped to talk to a nearby neighbour. This neighbour is a now a grandmother, and all her children are grown and live away from our small town. This neighbour is the kind of person who takes a genuine interest in others. Over the years that we have lived close by, she has watched our children grow through the first years of school to high school. In turn, we have noticed her family come home for major holidays, with their brood in tow. Knowing these neighbours as I do, I suspect that they did a pretty good job as parents. Nonetheless, in the midst of this brief street-side conversation, as the neighbour was asking how our children were doing, she said something like "I'm sure you know what to do with your kids, in our day we had to learn by the seat of our pants." The gist of what she was saying was that today we have so much information about parenthood, we should be able to feel more competent. She may also have been reflecting an expectation that, since my wife and I both work with children, she as a school principal and I as a psychologist, that we should know how to be exemplary parents. My wife's response to this was emphatic: "No, we don't, we don't know what we are doing! We are just trying to find our way in the dark like everyone else . . ." or words to that effect.

Even so-called experts in human relations can have problems with their personal relations: psychologists can have emotional problems; pastors, spiritual crisis.

There are no experts at home. Couples considering marriage, or partners in serious relationships thinking about having children, may generalize that because their partner gets along with their friends and work associates, that they will likely make a good parent. This isn't necessarily true, largely due to the emotionally laden nature of parenting relationships. Unlike work and friendship relationships, parenting is fraught with emotions, expectations and anxieties that can undermine any special expertise we think we have. This can be especially humbling for professionals, who, within the confines of their professional life, always seem to know what to do. It isn't as easy at home. This can lead to exaggerated guilt over mistakes they make as parents, or shame and embarrassment. Good parenting is a tight rope that few people walk without slipping. In a world where children can be damaged by too much closeness, as well as too much detachment, by over-interest as well as by neglect, what is likely most helpful will be certain attitudes and commitments. These include efforts to use social skills we graciously share with others, at home; a desire to continue to learn about parenting; the humility to admit mistakes and the grace to learn from them.

107

THE STRUCTURE OF HOME

amilies are like homes. They have a certain structure and some basic common components: living room, bedrooms, bathrooms, kitchen. The proportions and arrangement of these features is what gives houses their distinctiveness. In families, there are certain common components - adult to adult coalitions, sibling relations, rules and roles. How these are arranged changes the structure of families. Some people emerge from families that are highly structured. At the extreme, these families are rigid and authoritarian. Usually there is a very strong control by the parents in these homes. Expectations are clear and seldom change. In these families, parents often want to shield their children from life's hard lessons. At the extreme, this usually leads to massive conflicts in the teenage years. These families have been dubbed "brick wall families." In other homes, there is a tremendous amount of flexibility. At the extreme, these homes seem to be permissive. Children do pretty much as they please and parents think that it is best for kids to learn on their own. In other homes, there may appear to be to strict rules, but they are not enforced, or are enforced inconsistently.

When people are thinking about marriage and children, it is important to understand the kind of parenting structure their partner emerged from.

In really permissive families, there is an optimism that children need to have room to make mistakes because there is an expectation that they will learn from them. At their best, these families have a strong democratic theme. At their worst, they have been known as "jelly fish families," because they seem to lack back bone. Do any of these family shapes come near to describing the home you come from? When people are thinking about marriage and children, it is important to understand the kind of parenting structure their partner emerged from. Having similar backgrounds will likely help, since compatibility is a key component in marital adjustment. So you might think that couples who were raised in similar ways will not have problems with parenting. This doesn't apply, however, if you came from a family that had one of the dysfunctional structures, either the "jelly-fish" or the "brick wall" type. In this case, the couple will likely have to invest a considerable amount of time working out what was not helpful in their growing up. There are many great parent education programs, such as STEP (Systematic Training For Effective Parenting) and Active Parenting, that anyone could benefit from. There are also many good books, such as *How To Talk So Kids Will Listen & Listen So Kids Will Talk*. These things should be essentials for people who come from dysfunctional family structures, and for those who find themselves in a relationship with someone who was raised very differently.

Perplexing Problems, Troubling Times

REORGANIZING HURTING RELATIONSHIPS

Are there more problems in marriages today, or are they simply more openly reported? Most serious students of the family believe that a new ethic of openness about family life, combined with an enormous mass media, has meant that we are now, more than ever, aware of problems in family life. Turn the channel on your television and you can observe a talk show host talk to survivors of sexual abuse, wives whose husbands cheat on them, husbands whose wives are alcoholics: the list goes on and on. The theory goes that our most significant problems in family life - sexual abuse, domestic violence and alcoholism, have long been features of life for many families. Rather than things getting worse, people are now beginning to challenge these entrenched problems. More subtle than these massive social problems is the result of faulty communication styles, inappropriate parenting and low marital quality. All of these have a toll on human emotions. There are many relationships full of agony, hurt and desperation. And yet people hang in, hoping that things will improve, dedicated to the ideal of family stability. For example, Pauline is a woman who has recently left a marriage of over 20 years. She is plagued by feelings of failure and guilt. Her guilt is intensified by the fact that she feels free and at times happy to be out of a relationship in which she felt unloved and unsupported. Hurling one accusation after another against herself she said, "How could I break a marriage of over 20 years?" Today, Pauline wishes she would have confronted the problems within the marriage, earlier. But then, that's hindsight.

Knowledge about family problems seems to be teaching us one important lesson: relationship problems are seldom self-correcting.

In response, I asked her if perhaps the marriage had been broken for over twenty years, and throughout that time it was she who held it together. This seemed to make immediate sense to Pauline. As she looked back she could see that there were tremendous flaws in the marriage. They had shared a home, but never the intimacy she had hoped for. Like many women of our culture she hoped that one day things would change. She recalled that she had left her husband once when things got really bad. He beat her up then threatened suicide. She took him back out of fear. Some tolerate illegalities like abuse to keep a marriage together. The shocking truth is these things could have been predicted before marriage! The signs of relationship problems are often present from the beginning. The strategy of appeasement didn't help. You might say that it provided a veneer of family stability while they raised their kids. But there was a price tag. All we can do is use the best knowledge we have at the time. The proliferation of knowledge about family problems seems to be teaching us one important lesson: relationship problems are seldom self-correcting. You deserve to have relationships of love and respect. Anything less should be confronted, changed or discarded.

110

REORGANIZING TO SAVE THE MARRIAGE

Marilyn and Cecil are an interesting couple who have invested over five years in a second marriage. When they met, they both had kids. Their respective children seemed very accepting of the new relationship. After a brief courtship, they married and merged households and had a child of their own. Then their relationship fell victim to the number one problem in blended families: issues around parenting step-children. They made valiant efforts to solve the problem. They attended courses, they attended counselling, they made many a new start. Always, the triangle of natural parent, child and step-parent emerged as places of anger, hurt and misunderstanding. When they saw me for counselling, they had reached a point where divorce seemed the only option. In fact, they had booked their consultation with me to discuss how to buffer their children from the effects of the impending separation. I told Marilyn and Cecil about another couple I had known who had fallen in love when each was a single parent. Knowing that issues around step-parenting are a potential mine field, they choose to keep their own residences until their children were grown. They spent lots of time together, but hadn't cohabited. They seemed to have enough distance that the usual problems with step-children didn't materialize.

If it isn't working one way, reorganize, restructure, and invent.

When the children were grown, they were accustomed to the relationship and looked forward to the marriage. The point is, they didn't give their love relationship up because of the children: they sought an optimal organization of their family structure, without being bound by cultural expectations. When Marilyn and Cecil heard this story, they began to think that their initial response to their relationship problems had been too "all or nothing." They had laboured under the idea that they needed to share one roof to be married. The only alternative was divorce. The idea emerged that they too might find a way to reduce the amount of closeness and friction without giving up the love and connection they had. This was the curious thing about Cec and Marilyn: even though they had arrived for the consultation saying they were planning a divorce, they both said they loved the other and didn't want to give them up. So they decided to *reorganize*. Rather than accept the feelings of failure so often associated with divorce, they had seized the opportunity to try something new. They are going to try having separate residences, dates, many common meals and family times. They plan to keep their sexual relationship, one of the things they both enjoyed about their marriage. Likely the added distance will make them want each other all the more. Hopefully the conflict over parenting will be reduced. What they have discovered is something that more of us need to know, that we can be more creative in finding structures for our intimate relationships and families. If it isn't working one way, reorganize, restructure, and invent.

A SEXUALLY ABUSED SPOUSE

I t seemed like a straight forward case of marital alienation. She had lost interest, felt like she didn't love him anymore, couldn't see how she could go on pretending when the feelings weren't really there. Many couples come for counselling with this kind of scenario. The blame can be laid as much at the feet of the culturally prescribed roles for men and women, as it could be to either partner. Often she has not paid enough attention to her own needs, put his first, and he accepted. Years of inattention led to a crises. He wants the marriage fixed. She doesn't see how it can be. In this case, the lopsidedness of marriage had not been as pronounced. In fact, her husband had been pretty supportive and caring over the years. So where was the problem? While seeking an understanding of the couples' background, the therapist learns that she had been sexually abused as a child. Had she every received treatment for this? No. Did she think it was affecting her? No. Further exploration revealed that recent circumstances had placed the wife in a context reminiscent of the dynamics of her early home life and abuse - turns out that there was a mountain of feeling repressed about this. As the wife entered therapy, she began to see how this early abuse had pervasively affected her feelings about herself as a woman, her relationships, her ability to love and be sexual.

It may be hard to comprehend that one could be abused as a child and be in such denial that they have no recollection of it at all until it is triggered by some event in adult life, but it happens.

Very often the process of confronting the abuse and being healed is quite disruptive to normal functioning. There are periods of anger, depression and flat sexual desire. Since this has implications for marital relations, programs that treat adult survivors of sexual abuse often have a component which will help the spouse understand what their mate is going through. The main thing they need to do is be patient. Although there is no "average" treatment time, it is not unusual for healing to take a year or two. This will put a severe strain on the marriage unless the spouse is in some way involved in the treatment. It's strange that events we think are long past can return to plague us in adulthood. Discounting them as "done and forgotten" is more often a way of allowing these abuses to have uncontrolled, unconscious control over major decisions of our lives. In the case cited, facing them may not have saved the marriage, but was necessary for this woman to seize the kind of life she deserved. If you or your spouse has experienced sexual abuse, and you seem to be doing okay, this likely means you have a resilient personality. Nonetheless, it won't hurt your resiliency, and it may make a significant difference for the better if you explore this issue with the professional guidance of an accredited marriage and family therapist.

Affairs

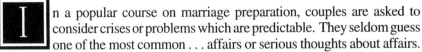 n a popular course on marriage preparation, couples are asked to consider crises or problems which are predictable. They seldom guess one of the most common . . . affairs or serious thoughts about affairs. Affairs, or serious thoughts about affairs, can mean many things. Popularly they are thought of as being immoral and something that only bad people do. The prevalence of affairs or serious thoughts of affairs, should lead one to think that there is something more to it that lack of moral fibre. Marriage therapists have long believed that affairs symbolize some lack of resolution of family or individual issues within one partner, or a dysfunction within a marriage. Often affairs, or serious thoughts of affairs, occur at transitions points in relationships, from childlessness to child bearing, from having kids to the empty nest. They are usually thought of as being part of a system, not an individual action. This meaning suggests that if the reasons for the affair are to disappear, something has to change in the marital context. This means that both parties, even the one not in the affair, would likely have to do some changing. Couples that weather these types of problems have many skills available. Foremost is the ability of the "offended" spouse to not personalize the affair or the disinterest of their partner. Although it may *feel* like a personal rejection, it usually isn't. If the "offended" spouse focuses on the perceived wrong done them, it will likely make matters worse.

**Note this page in the book, and if an affair happens in
your marriage, read it before you react!**

Instead they need to rise above this psychology of hurt and attempt to understand the *meaning* of the affair to their partner. What was missing? What were they looking for? Is it possible for them to have their needs met within the relationship? If the affair was a significant emotional matter, the offending spouse will likely go through a process of grief in relation to letting go of the affair. There may also be grief at a sense of loss of innocence or a loss of one's sense of self. It is important for the couple to know that as long as they are able to talk about these things, it is likely that they are healing the marriage by building intimacy again. To some degree it is predictable that at various times in a long term relationship partners will want to review their choice. It may mean that the relationship needs to change to fit emergent needs within the family context. The less open the process of reflection, the more likely the couple will be vulnerable to an affair or the equally distancing, thoughts of affairs. In the course on marriage preparation, couples are encouraged to face these problems by keeping their problem solving off the third party, and onto constructive honest discussion about their needs within the marriage. Note this page in the book, and if an affair happens in your marriage, read it before you react!

IN JOY AND IN SORROW

Have you ever attended a wedding and wondered if the people saying the vows to each other ever really reflected on what it is they are saying? In asking this, I don't mean to imply that people are cavalier about marriage. As a former clergyman, I officiated at a lot of weddings and I can't think of any marriages that weren't entered into without great sincerity. What I mean is that, even as they do reflect on their vows, it's unlikely that they could conceive of the meaning of certain phrases. One that comes to mind is "I take you in joy and in sorrow." Most young couples marrying would have to think that if all goes well, they will have to support each other through the loss of their parents. This is part of the predictable process of normal family life development. A generation passes away, a new one is born. These changes can add enormous stress to the structure of a marriage, as well as being a catalyst for growth. The death of one's parents can provoke a wide variety of emotional and intellectual changes. It can be a time of regret, heightened awareness of one's own mortality, and extreme loneliness. It can bring to the surface unresolved issues from one's childhood. Usually it is a time of sadness and re-connecting with other members of the family of origin. It is likely to upset the "quid pro quo," or the "something for something" in the marriage, or what sociologists of the family would call an imbalancing of the exchange of love services.

Let your partner handle their family their own way. A spouse can play an important support role when their partner loses a parent.

This type of life event challenges the maturity of the relationship and of the partners within it. It is important for the "in-law" spouse to be as involved as their spouse invites them to be. They may want time alone with their family, or they may want their partner to be intimately involved in the full process of the funeral and family grief process. It is never appropriate to make judgements about the person who has died, or about your partner's family, even if there is conflict. Don't take sides or attempt to interject your own views, whether it be your religious views or simply your views about cremation or the kind of funeral to have. Let your partner handle their family their own way. A spouse can play an important support role when their partner loses a parent. The most important thing is to give their partner time to grieve, not to resent or complain if they aren't fulfilling their usual roles. It is important not to be impatient with grief, which at times looks very similar to depression. As always, it important to be an empathic listener, putting aside more time than usual to connect and check in on the emotional climate of the spouse. Partners ready to do this, are likely prepared to say, "in joy and in sorrow."

ZERO TOLERANCE OF ABUSE

Zero tolerance for domestic violence. This means that when family violence occurs or is alleged, it is the obligation of the state to lay charges. It is no longer a matter of one family member charging another . . . it is now an offense that is of public concern. Zero tolerance for domestic violence suggests that there are no second chances, and no level of physical violence that be let pass. This kind of tough policy removes the abused person from the difficult role of having to be the main push for prosecution of their own family member. Manitoba has become the first province in Canada to institute such a "zero tolerance" policy. Critics of the plan suggest that the no tolerance policy leaves greater latitude for spurious allegations . . . that the less physically powerful (usually women) will gain a new legal club. A second criticism of zero tolerance of domestic abuse has to do with family members who are victims or witnesses of allegations of abuse, being in contempt of court if they refuse to testify when a case is brought to trial. For instance, a woman may call police for protection from an abusive spouse, then, as the trial approaches, for any number of reasons, decide that she does not want to testify. Should she face legal punishment? This could create the ironic situation of a victimized person being re-victimized by the state . . . someone without power again feeling powerless to determine their own course of action.

Despite the criticisms, zero tolerance of domestic abuse is likely a policy which in the long run will have a positive effect on family life.

It is known that many abused people abandon charges and that this is a part of the cycle of abuse. Even if they still are psychologically caught up in a system that will likely lead to re-offending, should the state force them to break this cycle? Despite the criticisms, zero tolerance of domestic abuse is likely a policy which in the long run will have a positive effect on family life. One can draw parallels from the field of sexual abuse studies, where the obligation of the state to investigate all reports of child sexual abuse has lead to a heightened sensitivity to what is acceptable and not in our society. Any child old enough to talk can allege that a caregiver has abused them. This can cause considerable embarrassment for a parent who has not abused, yet most parents are glad that children have this protection. Does this mean that children are now more powerful than parents? Not at all. The authorities are usually capable of sorting out legitimate cases from false. Even if the majority of charges are dropped, legal challenges can have a sobering effect. Like a line in the sand, zero tolerance provides an unequivocal message for family life: violence will *not* be tolerated as a means to settle family disputes.

115

NEW BOUNDARIES IN FAMILY LIFE

Holidays are a great time for visiting friends. This year I visited an old friend with a new problem. My friend was separated from his wife four years ago. Their separation had been civil, if not amicable. Issues of control and access to the children have strained the civility of their arrangement, however. Then, one day this summer, my friend went to pick up his children for his regular access, and they weren't home. He left notes on the front and back door for them to call when they got in. Later in the evening his ex wife called to say they were now home and although there was only a short time left in his access, that he could come over. His version of the story is that when he arrived, she had changed her mind. He could see his child in the kitchen and so entered the house to speak to her. His "ex" immediately called the police and alleged that he had assaulted her when she attempted to block his entrance to the house. My friend claims that this is a fabrication intended to assert her power in response to jealousy that he had now moved in with a new partner. The case has yet to go to court, but in the meantime the parental relationship is now thoroughly adversarial. If my friend is convicted, he faces exclusion from his professional association and the loss of his right to practice his profession. This case study of alleged domestic violence reveals the complexity of the issues.

Touching a person, without their consent, no matter our intent, may be experienced as an intrusion, and is not acceptable.

Foremost is the tremendous loyalty conflict in which the children must find themselves. The continuation of the working parental alliance is a major necessity if the negative impact of divorce is to be mitigated. Then there are the legal costs and the anxiety aroused by such a high stakes process. And what good will come of it? It seems to be a process fraught with winning and losing. Someone is bound to believe that they have been the victim of a miscarriage of justice. It is unclear how the main characters in this drama can benefit. Bystanders, like you and I, may stand to gain, if anyone can. We can learn something here about the new boundaries being enforced in families. Entering someone else's space without invitation, no matter the cause, may be experienced as a violation from which all persons are entitled to the protection of our society. These boundaries are the same no matter the intensity or nature of our relationship, whether we be family or stranger. This case also raises interesting questions, such as what are the boundaries between simple teasing and abuse? Between walking in and trespassing? How can society adjudicate the word of one adult against another? Who is a reliable witness in this emotionally laden incident? As a whole, as more such cases touch and trouble our lives, hopefully we will be helped to improve the overall quality of relationships in families and between the sexes.

BIBLIOGRAPHY

Arond, Miriam & Samuel L. Pauker *The First Year of Marriage* New York, N.Y.: Warner Books, c1987.

Beavers, W. Robert., *Successful Marriage: A Family Systems Approach To Couples Therapy.* New York. W.W. Norton & Co. 1985

Clinebell, Howard. *Basic Types of Pastoral Counselling* Abigon Press, New York, N.Y., 1966

Dinkmeyer, Don & Gary D. McKay *The Parents Handbook: Systematic Training For Effective Parenting* Circle Pines, Minn.: American Guidance Service, c1982.

Faber, A. & E. Mazlish, *How To Talk So Kids Will Listen & Listen So Kids Will Talk* New York: Rawson, Wade Publishers. c1980

Firestone, Robert. *Compassionate Child-Rearing: An In-depth Approach To Optimal Parenting.* New York, N.Y., Insight Books, c1990

Fogleberg, Dan *Longer* April Music Inc. 1979

Frankl, Victor Emil *Man's Search for Meaning.* New York, N.Y. Pocket Books, 1959

Fulghum, Robert. *All I Need To Know I Learned In Kindergarden: Uncommon thoughts on common thigs.* New York, N.Y., Villard Books, 1988

Gibran, Kahlil. *The Prophet.* New York, N.Y., Alfred A. Knopf, 1971

Harnick, Sheldon & Jerry Bock. *Fiddler on the Roof.* New York, N.Y., New York Times Music Corp., c1964

James, William. (1958) *The Varieties of Religious Experience* Mentor Books, New York.

Jipling, Zuo "Reciprocal Relationship between marital interaction and marital happiness: A Three-Wave Study." *Journal of Marriage and the Fami ly* November 1992

Lewis, Jerry M., Beavers, W. Robert., Gossett, Joh T., Phillips, Virginia Austin *No Single Thread: Pschological Health in Family Systems* New York. Bruner/Mazel

Mellan, Olivia. "The Last Taboo" *Family Therapy Networker* March/April 1992 p 41-47

Miller, Sherod., Nunnally, Elam., Wackman, Daniel. *The Couple Communica tion Instructor Manual* Interpersonal Communication Programs, Inc. Minneapolis, Minnesota, 1977

Nash, Richard *The Rainmaker* 1955

O'Connor, Dagmar *How To Make Love To the Same Person For the Rest of Your Life, and Still Love It!* Garden City, N.Y.: Doubleday,1985

Popkin, M., Gacia, E. & Woodward, H. *Active Parenting* Atlanta, Georgia: Active Parenting Inc.

Seligman, Martin E. P. *Learned Optimism* New York: A. A. Knopf, 1991

Shakespeare, William *Romeo and Julliet* London: Pan Books, 1972

Vannoy, Dana., Philliber, William W. "Wife's Employment and Quality of Marriage" *Journal of Marriage and The Family* May 1992 pp. 387-398.

ABOUT THE AUTHOR

Dr. Lees is a psychologist at the Chilliwack mental health centre and President of Integra Counselling Group Inc. He is author of *The Growth In Marriage Handbook*, has a regular radio feature *Notebook* on STAR-FM and is a clinical member of the American Association for Marriage and Family Therapy. In 1992 Dr. Lees was awarded the **Distinguished Service to Families Award** by the B.C. Council for the Family for his innovative work with couples and families. Dr. Lees resides in Chilliwack, B.C. with his wife and two children.

For more information on the PREPARE/ENRICH questionnaire please write or call:

In U.S.A.:   PREPARE/ENRICH
P.O. BOX 190
Minneapolis, MN 55440
Telephone   (612) 331-1731

In Canada: PREPARE/ENRICH
2024 St Albert Street
St. Albert, Alberta T8N 2G3
Telephone   (403) 973-3650
Fax   (403) 973-3850